THE CHRISTIAN WOMAN'S GUIDE TO DATING

The Christian Woman's

GUIDE to DATING

Advice on Keeping the Faith While Looking for Love

Selina Almodovar

ROCKRIDGE
PRESS

For general information on our other products and services or to obtain technical support, please contact our Customer Care Department within the U.S. at (866)744-2665, or outside the U.S. at (510) 253-0500.

Rockridge Press publishes its books in a variety of electronic and print formats. Some content that appears in print may not be available in electronic books, and vice versa.

All Scripture quotations are taken from the *Holy Bible*, New Living Translation, copyright © 1996, 2004, 2014 by Tyndale House Foundation. Used by permission of Tyndale House Publishers, Inc. Carol Stream, Illinois 60188, All rights reserved.

Interior and Cover Designer: Lindsey Dekker
Photo Art Director/Art Manager: Hannah Dickerson
Editor: Sam Eichner
Illustrations © Lena Nikolaeva/Shutterstock.com, cover; Basia Stryjecka/ Creative Market, p. V; All other illustrations used under license from North Sea Studio/Creative Market.

ISBN: Print 978-1-64739-693-0 | eBook 978-1-64739-694-7
R0

To Ky,
"Another one."

CONTENTS

INTRODUCTION

"Trust God."

That's what I tell my readers all the time. But if you knew me 15 years ago, you would be shocked to hear me say that so faithfully. Heck, I would be shocked, too.

Don't get me wrong. I've always loved the Lord. God has been a part of my life since I was a baby. I've always believed in God and identified myself as a Christian woman.

Back in my early dating days, however, I didn't listen to what God had to say. As a matter of fact, I was terrified of what God was saying—or, at least, of what His church was saying! I wasn't allowed to drink, smoke, get tattoos, have sex before marriage. There were so many rules to follow. And when it came to finding love, I broke all of them.

Each relationship I entered began with a "Hail Mary" prayer, begging God that *this* would be the guy to make all of my "happily ever after" dreams come true. And each time a relationship ended, I spiraled down a slippery slope of rejection, insecurity, and mistrust. I carried pain and anger in my heart for all of the guys who had hurt me. My faith was weak; I was often unforgiving. I would turn to alcohol and drugs to ease my pain, and though my Bible would lay open on my coffee table, God and His power had yet to pull me out of my misery.

That is, until my love life hit rock bottom: the moment when I finally grew sick and tired of letting my friends, my family, the internet, and romantic comedies hold sway over my heart. The advice I was receiving was not helping. Every relationship I'd gotten into made me feel worse about myself and this thing called "love." I had no choice. I turned to God.

Although it didn't happen right away, my decision to trust in God when it came to love was like lifting the shades to let the sunlight in. Slowly but surely, even as I continued to make poor relationship choices, God nudged me in His direction. He was showing me a better way to love.

Today's culture of dating and relationships can be brutal, particularly if your faith is a priority. The rise of internet pornography and hook-up culture—abetted by dating sites and apps—can make it harder than ever before to find and maintain a serious, healthy relationship. Yet, the internet has also opened up the modern dating world like never before, expanding the range of possibilities beyond chance run-ins with handsome guys at the gym or your local coffee shop. The common refrain that "there are no good guys left" leads women to believe it's slim pickings out there, which can result in lowered expectations and settling for subpar relationships. Believe me: I was there. I remember it like it was yesterday. As a single, Christian woman, I never once in a million years thought I could actually find a man whose values and beliefs aligned with mine. But it happened. And it can happen for you, too.

In this book, you'll discover that society—your friends, your family, your church—may not have given you a full picture when it comes to dating. Not only will this book address what it means to find love and sustain a relationship in today's world, it will do so in a way that's in harmony with your faith as a Christian.

To tackle love, sex, and dating, I will enlist the Word of God through Scripture, while also incorporating practical advice that's relevant to any modern woman. As such, this book is geared toward the devout Christian, who attends church every Sunday and is saving herself for marriage, as much as it is toward the casual Christian, who may not share in the traditional beliefs of the faith but still aligns herself with Christian values. From using God as a guide to set the right intentions and boundaries, to securing a first date, to leaning on Him for support when relationships don't pan out, this book will help you navigate every aspect of dating.

Why should you trust what I have to say about dating as a Christian woman? For starters, I'm not your average blogger. Through the combination of my writing, prayer books, relationship coaching services, and online courses, I've been able to deliver valuable insights to women around the world. Needless to say, I've been around the block once or twice when it comes to the intersection of dating, relationships, and faith.

Whether you're new to the dating scene or your love life has hit rock bottom (as mine did), it is my hope that this book will provide you with a clear sense of direction, belonging, and the affirmation that God is *for* you, not against you, in matters of the heart (Romans 8:31). No matter what life has thrown your way, my aim is to show you that a loving relationship is out there waiting for you, so long as you keep an open mind and a willing heart.

Above all, clothe yourselves with love, which binds us all together in perfect harmony.

COLOSSIANS 3:14

Chapter 1

LET LOVE IN

Love is everywhere. It's in the cartoons we absorb as kids and the movies we watch as adults. It streams from the stereos in our cars and peppers the pages of the books that line our shelves. And it's on our minds when we meet someone who gives us butterflies. But with the exciting prospect of romantic love comes the inevitable fear of love's scorn. In this chapter, we'll welcome love into our lives by achieving a greater understanding of what love is, where it actually comes from, and how dating can help us find it.

WHAT IS LOVE?

We all know the story of the beautiful princess who, through a series of misadventures, ends up in the loving arms of a handsome prince, living out her happy ending in a majestic castle in a far-off land (or, if the tale is set in a modern romantic comedy, a well-appointed New York City apartment). I don't know about you, but besides thinking I could sing, dance, look, and feel like a princess, I dreamed of someday finding that fairy-tale kind of love.

Let me tell you, that was not the love I got. In fact, my experience with love was far from the typical fairy tale. Turns out, those stories hadn't taught me anything about real love. Sure, I dated a few beasts in my time, but those relationships never turned into happily-ever-afters. Quite the opposite. And in light of those disappointments, I started to feel less and less confident that this magical thing we call love even existed.

Although you were likely taught about love your entire life, I'm willing to guess the sources were untrust-worthy. In order to find and experience true love, we need to wipe away the make-believe and uncover what it means to be truly loved (spoiler alert: There are no singing animals).

The truth about love—*real* love—is that it comes from God. He is the very essence of love, and if you read His Word, you will discover that everything He did was an act of love. God and the Bible teach us not only how *to* love but also how we should *be* loved. Now, you're free to stick to the "princess state of mind," hoping against hope that some Prince Charming will one day find you. But if you're ready to explore the truth behind what true love is and how you can find it in your own life, let's take a deeper look at the characteristics of love God has already revealed to us through His Word.

Love Is Sacrifice

But anyone who does not love does not know God,
for God is love. 1 JOHN 4:8

Do you know where the very first mention of "love" appears in the Bible? It is found in Genesis 22:1–2, when God instructs Abraham to take his son, Isaac, "whom he loves," and offer him as a sacrifice to Himself. You're probably thinking that biblical sacrifice has absolutely nothing to do with dating, right? Well, let's take a closer look.

Do you think it's a coincidence that the very first mention of love in the Bible is used in the very same terms in which God offered his Son, Jesus, whom He loves, as a sacrifice for us? I don't. In fact, it shows us that the greatest love of all is God's love for us as His children.

Think about it: God doesn't initially explain love when Eve first met Adam—a relational love. Instead, He breaks it down by sharing how a father is willing to sacrifice his son to prove his love and devotion to God—a sacrificial love. Ultimately, God wants us to love each other not only relationally, but also sacrificially.

Using God's sacrificial love as a blueprint, we can allow love to become more present in our own lives. Everything God has ever done for us has been out of love. Every time we choose to express an act of love, we are doing so because God demonstrated how to do it first.

If you want to know how to love and how to recognize love, the best model is in the reflection of God. Are you questioning whether you should be dating a particular guy? Ask yourself: Is the man you're dating showing you a love that resembles how Jesus taught His church to love? Is he willing to make significant sacrifices for you and the relationship? If so, chances are he's a keeper.

Love Is Unconditional

> *Even before he made the world, God loved us and chose us in Christ to be holy and without fault in his eyes. God decided in advance to adopt us into his own family by bringing us to himself through Jesus Christ. This is what he wanted to do, and it gave him great pleasure. So we praise God for the glorious grace he has poured out on us who belong to his dear Son.* EPHESIANS 1:4–6

We tend to believe that love is a conditional thing. That relationships fail because one or both parties believe their love for the other is bound up in would-be acts of kindness or sacrifice. That if he *really* loved you, he would do whatever it is you want him to do. Or conversely, that if you could just transform yourself into the woman you think he wants you to be, he would *really* love you in turn.

But that's not how God shows us to love. His love for us has no contingency plan; it persists whether we mess up or not. As you can see from the passage from Ephesians, He chose us way before anything else ever happened—way before Adam and Eve ever sinned. Indeed, Jesus became the solution to the sin that would separate us from God and His love the very day that He dismissed the serpent from the Garden of Eden (Genesis 3:15). Jesus was a part of the plan all along. Why did God choose us from the very beginning? Because He loves us. And He wants us to love Him, too.

This does not mean that God will only love you once you get your life together or after you've lost a bit of weight. God loves you just as you are, however you are, simply for being you. Once you start dating someone and your love for each other grows, the same notion should apply. That person should love you simply for being you, not for who you will one day become.

When you choose to marry someone, you should be at a point in your relationship where your love for your partner is just like God's love for us: unconditional. As you make your vows, you are promising to love him "for better or worse, in sickness and in health, for richer or poorer." Those terms spell out a "no matter what" kind of love. As in, no matter what happens in life, you are promising to love this man! And, equally important, this man is promising to love you unconditionally, with no strings attached.

Love Is Immeasurable

And I am convinced that nothing can ever separate us from God's love. Neither death nor life, neither angels nor demons, neither our fears for today nor our worries about tomorrow—not even the powers of hell can separate us from God's love. No power in the sky above or in the earth below—indeed, nothing in all creation will ever be able to separate us from the love of God that is revealed in Christ Jesus our Lord. ROMANS 8:38–39

God's love has no limits. It doesn't matter what you do, what you say, whom you date, or whom you choose to love—God will never, ever stop loving you. His very being is love, and as He created you in His image, you have been designed to love Him back. As such, you, too, possess an immeasurable amount of love to give and receive freely. No matter what you do, you will never run out of love to give to someone.

Have you ever been afraid to love someone because you thought that if you got your heart broken, you wouldn't be whole enough to love the right guy whenever he came along? Do you ever fear that you loved too much in the past and won't have enough love for the future? Have you ever loved someone so much that you believed it impossible to love like that again? If you answered "yes" to any of those questions, I have good news for you: If you are choosing to love like God, the well of your love is infinitely deep.

What God has taught us is that there is no limit to how much love you can give, receive, and have within yourself. This is why it is so easy to love friends, family members, pets, and the men who come into your life. If you fear that your love has been depleted by a past relationship, fear not: The love you will need to give to someone new will come! We are permanently inseparable from God's love, and we will always have enough of it to pour into ourselves and others.

Love Is Essential

We love each other because he loved us first.
1 JOHN 4:19

As Christians, it is extremely important to love simply because God loves us. It's what we were created to do. Above all else, we are commanded to love the Lord with all our heart and to love others as we love ourselves (Matthew 22:36–40). In order to seek the happiness and fulfillment that we long to feel from a romantic, lifelong relationship, it's essential to lead a life full of love.

Whenever you feel like love is absent from your life, take a second look. While you may only be paying attention to certain kinds of love, such as romantic love, a life of love extends way beyond your most intimate relationship. God has already given us a life of love because He has already chosen to love us. Love is not something you acquire or earn after having successfully been in a relationship long enough. Love is essential to live a happy and healthy life, period.

Let's break this down: Because God loves us first and foremost, He opens doors for us to receive love all the time. This love can come in many forms: provisions, health, professional opportunities, and relationships, platonic or otherwise. And because we feel and receive this love from God, we can funnel it back into the people and passions that fill us with love, loving through acts of service (such as taking care of others or our environment), our creations (what we make with our talents, skills, and innovative minds), and our relationships (how we choose to love others).

But remember: Although God's love will always be present, a life of love cannot happen unless we allow it to happen.

Love Is a Choice

> *But to all who believed him and accepted him,*
> *he gave the right to become children of God.*
> JOHN 1:12

By now, you should know that God's love is the real deal! And once you accept that kind of love into your life, you can channel it into just about everything you do. As we've discussed, God's love is unconditional and immeasurable. Sounds like the very best kind of love you should be looking for from the very best kind of man, right?

But there is one major element worth stressing before we go any further: You have to *choose* to receive God's love. Even though God chose to love you a long time ago, you still have to choose to accept and adopt God's love into your own life. As long as we believe in Him and are accepting Him as our God, we are *choosing* to be His children (John 1:12).

Not everyone chooses to receive the love of Christ. Likewise, not everyone chooses to live a life full of love.

It's probably why those fairy tales seem so glamorous at first, only to come up short when you project them onto your own love life. God's love becomes real to us when we choose to receive it.

The best way to receive God's love is simply to ask for it. Try saying this prayer out loud whenever you feel the desire to love the way that God has shown you to love:

Dear God,

Thank you for loving me without limits or conditions. There are times when I forget that Your love is always there for me to receive and use to love myself and others. Help me be mindful of Your everlasting, unconditional, immeasurable love. Show me every day what it means to love like You. I ask that You open my heart, come live inside of it, and help me live the rest of my days loving You, myself, and others just as You have done for me.

Amen.

WHY DATE TO FIND LOVE?

If God's love is the best kind of love out there, why even try to find love through dating? Simply put: God not only created you to love Him, He also created you to love *others*. It's in your makeup to want to love someone else. Just as God created Eve to live alongside Adam in the Garden of Eden, the desire to find your lifelong partner has been in your heart for as long as you can remember!

However, dating and Christianity don't always mix. You may be familiar with certain Christian lifestyles, which dictate that you have to date in very particular ways (such as no kissing before marriage); that you should "wait to date" until you know for sure that the person you date is the one you will marry; or worse, that you shouldn't be dating at all because doing so could open the doors to temptation, leave your heart exposed, or lead you to fall for the wrong guy.

I get that certain fears of dating can make you want to avoid the matter altogether. But dismissing the concept of dating will not alleviate your desire to find love in a potential lifelong partner. It may seem like dating in this day and age could conflict with your Christian beliefs and values. For example, when trying to find someone to date, you may feel like you need to dress provocatively when you prefer to dress modestly, or drink on dates when you don't drink. But what if dating was, instead, done with God's guidance? Moreover, what if dating could actually deepen your faith and relationship with God?

What follows are the ways in which dating can actually help you become a stronger and more spiritual Christian.

Dating Helps You Understand Yourself Better

God calls us to love others. But in order to love others, we must first love ourselves. And while dating, by definition, implies finding someone else to love, the journey can help us discover how to love ourselves as well.

One of the greatest commandments, after loving the Lord with all of your heart, is to love others *as yourself* (Matthew 22:36–40). But how can you love others as yourself if you don't know how to love yourself? Who you are when you are alone, versus who you are when you are around others, could be two completely different people. But if you're comfortable being true to yourself, regardless of who you're with, you'll be much more equipped to notice when something is causing you to change, particularly when that "something" is the person you're dating.

On the other hand, who you are when you are single can differ from who you are once you start dating. What better way to learn more about yourself and the woman that God is calling you to be than to understand who you are when you enter into a close relationship with someone else? In this new dynamic, you can discover your limits (what you can and can't stand), your values (what really matters to you), and what you long to have in your future (marriage, children, a career, etc.).

Although you may think you can figure all this out on your own or through experiences with your close friends and family, the fact remains that your attitude and desires change once you place yourself in a dating situation. Your friends, for example, will not challenge you the same way a suitor or boyfriend might. Ultimately, dating is just practice for the big game: a real, serious, loving relationship. It is the means by which you can better understand who you are and what you want so that, when the right guy comes a-calling, you'll be confident enough to decide he's the one worth spending your life with.

Dating Can Allow You to Redouble Your Devotion to God

Some women believe dating will divert their attention away from God and their devotion to Him. In fact, this is one of the primary reasons dating has such a tainted reputation within the Christian community. But if you choose to date with God on your side, dating can actually redouble your devotion to Him.

God's Word instructs you to, "Trust in the Lord with all your heart; do not depend on your own understanding. Seek his will in all you do, and he will show you which path to take" (Proverbs 3:5–6). By sharing your dreams and desires to date with God and choosing to trust in Him to make that opportunity possible, you are relying on God to deliver on your romantic prospects. By trusting in God to create a suitable man for you, you are trusting that God knows the desires of your heart and will direct your path toward finding him, even if that path involves a few twists and turns.

As you make efforts to find someone who is actually worth spending time with, hold on to the hope that someone will someday arrive through God's will. During this time, continue seeking the Lord for His wisdom and direction on the matter. When things don't go the way you had hoped, you can lean on God and not simply your own understanding. In this way, faith is rebuilt. And when it's time to start dating again, having faith in God means having faith that what He has planned for you will eventually inspire you to get back out there.

Dating Is an Opportunity to Learn How to Communicate Better with Others

Everyone has their own opinion. Not everyone will speak the same love language as you or approach a problem the same way. Not everyone will agree with everything you say and do, whom you vote for, or which church is the best place for worship. Everyone has a different say on different matters for different reasons, some of which you may never understand. And those differences can lead you to make snap judgments and form preconceived notions if you let them.

God teaches us, however, to treat others who may have different opinions with love and respect. His Word tells us to, "Understand this, my dear brothers and sisters: You must all be quick to listen, slow to speak, and slow to get angry" (James 1:19). This may be an easy thing to do when you're choosing to talk to people with whom you're already familiar, but when you're on a date and trying to get to know someone on a deeper level, it can prove quite challenging. God instructs us to be mindful of others' thoughts and needs; when we are, we genuinely learn more about them, as opposed to solely focusing on ourselves and our own assumptions.

In short, dating can be a great way to connect with others who may be different from yourself in terms of their faith, upbringing, values, and more. It can provide an avenue to speak like Christ—to be open and accepting of others, while tactfully expressing your own thoughts and opinions. Typically, the success of a date is determined by the quality of the conversation. But even if you decide to never date someone again, communicating with that person should always come from a place of love—God's love.

Dating Can Encourage You to Take Action in Faith

If you like someone and pray to God that they like you back, but then you fail to actually *do* something about it, it's likely that special someone will not seriously pursue you (at the very least, a text back is required!). While we'll talk more about what to do when you actually like someone and start to date in chapter 4, it's critical to combine the faith you have in God's plan with action.

The Bible tells us that "faith by itself isn't enough. Unless it produces good deeds, it is dead and useless" (James 2:17). In other words, even if God is opening doors for you to get to know someone or to go on a date, you still need to walk through those doors!

The fear of failure, heartbreak, or humiliation you may have stored away from past dates or relationships can be so paralyzing that you don't act at all. But this inaction is not of God. After all, "We can make our plans, but the Lord determines our steps" (Proverbs 16:9).

Dating may take you out of your comfort zone, but rest assured, it is in those moments that God's hand can be most acutely felt, as He molds you into the person He planned on you becoming. If you want dating to help you become a stronger Christian, then you may have to take a few leaps of faith, like saying "yes" to dates or simply texting the guy you're interested in rather than waiting for him to text you. Doing so will help you find and establish the kind of relationship God has designed for you.

Dating Can Bring You Closer to Finding God's Perfect Gift for You

At the end of the day, dating can be the stepping-stone to finding a husband. Of course, marriage is a part of God's original design. In His Word, God says, "'It is not good for the man to be alone. I will make a helper who is just right for him'" (Genesis 2:18). What's important to note here is the phrase, "who is just right for him." In other words, God has created a wife (you) uniquely fit for the needs of your future husband, and vice versa.

If you believe in God's love and you are choosing to date under the guidance of His truth, you should also believe that God will call on you to become your husband's "perfect gift" and on your husband to become yours. Each of you is designed to complement and serve the needs and wants of the other. It's almost too good to be true!

Dating is, of course, the first step of the journey toward building an exclusive relationship with the man God has created for you. Without dating, this man may never get to know you well enough to love you beyond the friendship level. Dating is the entryway to the course God has charted for you.

Sure, you may have to date multiple people before finding the right person, but you don't have to have a heart and soul connection with each and every man you date. What dating can do is show you that God was thinking of you all along—that, in spite of any obstacles He threw your way, He was simply sending you down a path to the person you'd been looking for all along.

Insights and Affirmations

Insights

- Dating will not pull you away from your devotion to God, unless you allow it to.
- You can use God's love as a blueprint of what to look for when loving and receiving love from others.
- What leads to a happy, fulfilled marriage is learning how to love like God.

Affirmations

- Dating (as we understand it today) does not exist in the Bible! Only God's truth when it comes to loving Him and loving others does (see Matthew 22:36–40).
- God's love is everywhere—in all things and for all people—and you must choose to receive it (see 1 John 4:7–8).

No one hates his own body but feeds and cares for it, just as Christ cares for the church. EPHESIANS 5:29

Chapter 2

DATING STARTS WITH YOU

Dating is a tale of two souls attempting to forge a connection—to cultivate happiness and fulfillment within each other, through each other. It's a dance, and once you find that ideal dance partner, you'll hope the soundtrack to your relationship never ends.

Yet, in order to perform this delicate two-step, you have to show up knowing your part. In other words, you have to show up knowing *yourself*. Realizing who you really are, what you actually want, and how you need to be loved is all part of the rehearsal. Once you figure that part out, the way you view dating, love, and relationships will change. In this chapter, you'll see why understanding (and loving) yourself is essential to effectively identifying the kind of person you want as your lifelong dance partner.

LOVE YOURSELF FIRST

I used to be the perfect girlfriend. I was kind. I would make meals for my boyfriends. I would encourage them to go after their dreams. I always went above and beyond to meet their needs.

I also used to agree with everything they said. I would dress to cater to their style. I would listen to all the music they wanted to listen to. I would eat all of their favorite foods. I avoided arguments. Whenever their family and friends were around, I was the model girlfriend. And yet, these relationships never worked out.

When the breakups came, they left me devastated. I thought I had it all figured out. What did I do wrong? If I was the "perfect girlfriend," what could possibly be missing?

In retrospect, the answer was as obvious as it was mystifying: It was me. *I* was missing. I had removed myself—*my* wants, *my* needs, *my* interests—from the equation to such an extent that I didn't even know who I was without my partner. Once these relationships ended, I was left feeling completely devastated, lost, and afraid to be alone.

As a result, I spent the majority of my single life trying to figure out who I really was. It may not come as a shock to you, but knowing who you are is *pretty* important to dating. If you don't know who you are, how could anyone else ever possibly get to know you well enough to love you the way you deserve to be loved?

It may sound cliché, but it's true: The only way to find someone worthy of your love is to love yourself first.

It wasn't until I discovered who I really was—and, get this, *accepted* who I was—that I was able to fully let someone in and love me the way I needed to be loved. All those other guys, they were simply following my lead. Because I didn't show love toward myself, they didn't show love toward me, either. Because I was totally engulfed in them and their needs, they were consumed in themselves and their needs, too. To be loved, you need to express self-love and live a life that demonstrates that love. Trust me, when you do, it becomes a whole lot easier to tell when you're wasting your time with someone who doesn't genuinely love you for you.

Of course, society doesn't always make it easy for us women to love ourselves. The pressure to look, dress, and act a certain way can be overwhelming (God forbid you don't have eyelash extensions and know how to contour in time for your first date!). We live in a day and age where social media takes our best pictures and attaches them to likes and follows. Ingrained in us every time we pick up our phones is the notion that only the "best" versions of ourselves are really worth anyone's attention.

Don't sacrifice yourself in service to this lie! Remember: Who you are is who God designed you to be. Your smile, your dreams, your tastes, what you find funny (and what you don't)—all are traits you should love about yourself, regardless of who else loves them.

When all is said and done, the love you have for yourself is going to be the strongest, most attractive thing about you. But first things first: Do you actually love yourself? How would you even know?

To help you find out, here are some tips on how you can practice self-love.

Make a vision board. Take time to thoughtfully curate images that are representative of your short- and long-term dreams and goals and create a vision board that you can reflect upon when you feel uninspired or lost.

Create an environment that you love to be in. Redecorate your room, give your home a makeover, or redesign your office space so that you feel at peace in the places you spend the most time.

Establish a morning routine that allows you to focus on your physical and mental well-being. Start your day off disconnected from your phone. Enjoy a cup of coffee or tea, meditate, or do a workout/yoga routine. Journaling or spending time doing a devotional are also great ways to set your mind, body, and spirit on the right track as you start your day.

Don't hesitate to seek counseling. If you're financially able, reaching out to a therapist to help you work through any unresolved issues or painful past experiences can be life changing.

Select one hobby to focus on each year. Dedicate time each week to enjoying the hobby and improving your skills.

Find a fitness routine. Working out regularly can boost your mood and relieves stress. Achieving your ideal body shape and size is just a perk!

Connect with your closest friends each month. Make a point of catching up with your closest friends at least every other week or month for a meal or coffee. Make time to go out with them, have fun, and try new things together.

Create a personal skincare and haircare routine. Develop a routine for your skin and hair that helps you take the very best care of your natural self.

Get enough sleep every night and on the weekends. Try to take an hour before bed to start your nighttime routine. Set yourself up for the following morning, take a shower or bath, do your nighttime skincare regimen, and make sure that your bedroom is a sanctuary for sleep.

Set up a daily habit of connecting with God through prayer, church, worship, or meditation. Follow a daily Bible reading plan; journal your daily prayers each morning; or listen to a worship playlist, faith-based podcast, or church sermon.

What's the Word?

Thank you for making me so wonderfully complex! Your workmanship is marvelous—how well I know it.
PSALM 139:14

Blood orange sunsets. Sprawling fields of wildflowers. Shimmering oceans and lakes. Just as you wouldn't expect Picasso to create an average work of art, you shouldn't expect the same God responsible for all that natural splendor to create you any differently. You are fearfully and wonderfully made! Let that sink in as you start to address the love that you have for yourself. God loved you enough to make you *you*, from the texture of your hair, to the shape of your toes, to the sound of your laugh, to the things you're most passionate about.

Everything that makes you who you are has been orchestrated within you for a purpose. God thinks you're marvelous. And there is someone great out there who will agree. Do you see what God sees in you? Start loving yourself the way God does and the way you long to be loved by someone else.

IDENTIFY YOUR VALUES

One surefire way to love and respect yourself, and incorporate that love and respect into a relationship, is to be aware of your values. At the end of the day, what is most important to you? Who matters most? What are your deal makers? And, equally important, what are your deal breakers?

Once you've identified your values, you can more effectively discern whether they are being honored by your partner. Clear indications that your partner honors your values are signs that a relationship has legs; if the opposite is true, it may be time to find someone who does.

When your values are missing from your dating experience, your judgment becomes foggy and messy. You start to focus on all of the wrong reasons why you should continue to date someone, and when your values finally reenter the equation, it may be too late.

So, let's face this head-on. In the pages to follow, I've compiled a (incomplete) list of personal values. Take a minute to read it over. Then, prioritize them. You can even write them out on a sheet of paper and rank them. Which values are most important to you and how you live your life? Which values are less crucial? With regard to a partner, on which values are you willing to be flexible? On which values are you intransigent?

Before you get started, I implore you to be mindful of your faith and of how important God's love is to you. Not every man you meet is going to be on the same spiritual path as you. While you both may believe in God, you may approach your faith in different ways.

Be sure to take this into consideration when evaluating your values.

Family: Is having kids something you see for yourself? How meaningful is it to include extended family into your lifestyle?

Friendship: Do you need to live a lifestyle that regularly incorporates close friends? Is it important for you and your partner to have shared friends? How important is it to maintain relationships with people in your extended network, such as friends from church, work, and other places?

Honesty: How important is it for you to be able to speak honestly about your thoughts and opinions with the person you love? Do you need to feel and know that you are accepted as you are?

Independence: Do you need to have the ability to go out and do whatever you want, when you want, without strict restrictions from a partner, work, money, and other pressures?

Tradition: Do you cherish upholding family, personal, or faith-based traditions? Is teaching and sharing your traditions with others something you value in your life?

Diversity: Is it important for you to be surrounded by a diverse group of people and opinions? How important is it for you to be engaged in these kinds of settings?

Security: When placed in an environment, how emotionally, physically, and/or mentally grounded do you need to feel? How important is this feeling of security to the health of a relationship?

Emotional intelligence: How important is it for you to be able to address various emotional conflicts with respect and tact? How important is it for a partner to do the same?

Health and wellness: How much do you value a willingness and ability to care for one's mental and physical wellness through eating healthy, exercising, meditating, praying, and the like?

Work-life balance: Are you able to separate yourself from your work when you're at home (and from home while you're at work)? How vital is it for you and your partner to maintain this balance?

Professional achievements: How important to you is a feeling of professional fulfillment? What might you be willing to sacrifice for your job or an advancement in your career?

Education: Is one's level of education important to you? Or does someone's education not factor into your evaluation of their intelligence?

Desire to learn: Do you find that having a desire to constantly learn and grow is something you admire in others and need in your own life?

Stability: How important is it for you (and a potential mate) to keep a steady job and consistent schedule? Do you need to settle down in one place? Or are you willing to relocate under the right circumstances?

Financial wealth and status: How important is financial wealth to you? How important to you is it to live within a particular socio-economic class or community?

Is it a factor in determining the suitability of a potential mate? Do you value a lifestyle that allows you to pay down your debt, save money for your future, and live where money is not a major stressor in your life? Under what circumstances might you make exceptions?

Social life: How important is it for you to engage socially with others by enjoying experiences outside of your home? What kind of experiences do you enjoy? Are you a social drinker? How critical is it that your partner's social preferences align with yours?

Church: Do you value a lifestyle that allows you to attend regular weekly church services? Is it crucial for you to attend church at least once a week? How important is it for you to invest your time and attention toward a particular ministry (such as joining the worship team, community outreach, or teaching Sunday School) within the church?

Spiritual growth: Is engaging in moments of personal prayer important to you? Is the interest and/or desire to study the Bible a feature of your life? Does it matter to you that you are learning more about God on a consistent basis?

Serving others: How important to you is it to give your time to serve the needs of others, particularly those less fortunate?

Now that you have a better sense of your
values and which ones mean the most to you,
take a look at the list again. If there is a value
you wish to acquire or strengthen, now is as
good a time as any to start. Here are some
tips for getting the ball rolling:

1. *Once you've prioritized the values on this*
   list and added any that may've been miss-
   ing, select a value you'd like to focus on.

2. *Set a goal for yourself within the context*
   of that value. This could be anything from
   connecting with your family more, to get-
   ting in better physical shape, to decreasing
   your financial debt.

3. *Now, write down three to five actionable*
   steps you can take to achieve your goal
   over the next year. Then, break those steps
   down even further into "baby steps" you
   can take each month.

STAYING TRUE TO YOUR FAITH

While we're on the subject of upholding your values, let's
not forget about your faith! Last I checked, the Bible
does not contain any specific rules for dating. That said,
you can certainly find some advice in there on protecting yourself from temptation and establishing clear

boundaries to shield yourself emotionally, physically, sexually, and spiritually.

Christian or not, we all maintain a particular set of boundaries to stop ourselves (and others) from going too far. Some women opt to protect their sexual purity by saving themselves for marriage; others who value their mental purity may choose not to watch R-rated movies; others still may choose not to talk to anyone in the morning until they've spent some time alone, meditating, praying, or otherwise focusing on their emotional or spiritual well-being. In short, your values are important and worth protecting, particularly when you're in the process of opening up your heart to finding love. Boundaries make that possible.

Not everyone you date will understand this. If they do not value the same things as you, they may attempt to cross your boundaries. To enforce them, you can choose to be honest and up-front about your choices and explain why the boundaries are in place; this can be difficult, as it is easy to get swept up in the wants and whims of someone you like. You can also put some distance between yourself and the person you're dating as a means of helping you regain your sense of perspective. Those who really know you and care about your well-being can help you uphold your values and remind you when the walls you've put up to protect them are crumbling. Use your friends as a support system. Encourage them to ask you frequently about your boundaries, discuss those that require maintenance, and continue to check in as your relationship progresses.

The result of relinquishing your boundaries—of continuously letting someone you're dating cross the line and diminish the values you're trying to protect—can have injurious effects not only on your relationship, but also on your faith and sense of self.

Here are a number of common consequences associated with boundary-crossing.

You place their needs and wants above your own. Instead of focusing on what's best for you, you aim to please your partner and always put them first.

You end up compromising your own identity. You start to forget about yourself—your likes, dislikes, and values—all over again.

Your partner loses respect for your values. If you do not honor your own values, you tacitly show your partner that it's okay for them to not honor your values, either. Soon, your values will become unimportant.

You start working harder in the relationship than your partner. Because you want to make your relationship last *and* reestablish your boundaries, you can end up working overtime.

You ease up on other boundaries. Once you allow one important boundary to be crossed, it becomes increasingly difficult to enforce others.

You struggle to honor the value(s) the boundary was meant to protect. Because you've already crossed the boundary, it would seem weird to pretend it didn't already happen. This tension makes it difficult to return to square one.

You feel let down and ashamed for not being able to honor your own values. Since you've allowed yourself to believe that you are incapable of setting a boundary for yourself, you may start to believe that what you set out to do is impossible.

You may not get to experience what the relationship could have been like if your values were upheld and respected. Once a boundary that was meant to protect you and your values has been crossed, you will never know what the relationship could have been like had that boundary never been crossed to begin with.

It can be difficult to set rules and boundaries for yourself in dating and other aspects of life. But they are there to protect the things that matter most—in this case, not just your core values, but also your faith in God and the woman He is calling you to be.

THE BEAUTY OF OPENNESS

Throughout this chapter, I've tried to impress upon you the importance of loving yourself, protecting your values, and maintaining the integrity of your faith. But let's not conflate these truths with the notion that you should be closed off to new ideas, places, activities, and people. In fact, the opposite is true: The more confident you are in yourself and your values, the more comfortable you'll be with opening yourself up to new experiences.

Sometimes, we conjure up an idea of what we want a relationship to look like or how we want the next person we date to be. On dating websites, matchmaking services, and apps, we increasingly filter the field

Practical Wisdom: How to Say "No"

In order to stay true to yourself and not compromise your values for the sake of someone else, you should have a clear and direct plan for how and when to say "no." For starters, do not worry about disappointing or upsetting someone else. Be very clear and up-front. A simple "No, we're not going there" is usually all you need to reiterate your boundaries. If they don't get the message, even after you've explained why you've set them, or if they try to protest, disengage yourself from the situation. Period. Hang up, leave the room, or otherwise shut down the conversation.

This may feel awkward, but that's not your fault. You didn't make it awkward by saying "no"; the other person made it awkward by trying to do something they knew you weren't comfortable with. Stand up for yourself when no one else will. Love yourself first!

of potential suitors through this idea, eliminating men on the basis of preferences attached to a concept of who we think we want to date. Yet limiting yourself to a "type" can impede you from finding the person who is actually right for you; it can also challenge your willingness to follow and trust God's direction. It's hard to find the right person if you're not open to the world and all it has to offer. As the saying goes, love may very well come when you least expect it.

In truth, the type of guy you have in mind may not take into account all of the things God sees and knows about you and your needs. Moreover, the places and experiences you are used to will not pull you out of your comfort zone and toward a place of growth.

In the Bible, God Himself declares, "'My thoughts are nothing like your thoughts . . . And my ways are far beyond anything you could imagine. For just as the heavens are higher than the earth, so my ways are higher than your ways and my thoughts higher than your thoughts'" (Isaiah 55:8–9).

To put it another way: You have no idea what God is getting ready to do for you—in your love life or with the next man you meet and decide to date. Approaching the dating scene with an open mind can be exactly what God wants you to do!

Naturally, this is easier said than done. Keeping an open mind and being vulnerable forces you to let down your guard in certain areas. It may require you to place yourself in a position where you could get hurt or judged—even "ghosted" (see page 67). Nobody said dating was easy, but it's worth the risk if you do it under God's guidance.

Do your best to explore what it means to be open in a safe and constructive way. Without bending your boundaries or dismissing who you are as an individual, try saying "yes" to suitors and date ideas that you might not normally agree to. If there's something you've never tried before but always wanted to, a date is a great excuse to try it. Experiencing something new with someone new can help bring you closer together. Be open to giving the nice guy a chance, even if you've already crossed him off your list for being "too nice." Be open to going on a date with a man who's shorter than you'd prefer. Be open to someone who may not be as educated as you'd like, at least on paper. Don't shy away from dancing, singing, laughing, and loving the skin you're in; it may make you feel uncomfortable at first, but you'll soon discover that opening yourself up to the world can lead you to places you've never been before—not to mention, to men you may never have met otherwise.

And always remember: God is your guiding light. Use His truth to direct your steps. And trust in His nudges when He tells you it's time to take a step in faith.

Insights and Affirmations

Insights

- Change the dating game by understanding who you are and what you need to be fully loved.
- The values you protect will serve as the building blocks of your relationship. Weak values make for a weak relationship.
- Boundaries are beautiful, especially when they're established to serve your inner and outer beauty. Allow them to help you grow more comfortable with experiencing new things and meeting new people.

Affirmations

- God made you special and different from everyone else. You are truly one of a kind (Psalm 139:14).
- God's ways are not your ways. If you are looking to God to bring someone into your life worth dating, remember that He's going to do it in His own way, not yours (see Isaiah 55:8–9).

Don't copy the behavior and customs of this world, but let God transform you into a new person by changing the way you think. Then you will learn to know God's will for you, which is good and pleasing and perfect. ROMANS 12:2

Chapter 3

SET YOUR SIGHTS

Ever watch a movie or television show and start to picture yourself in the scenario with the love interest? Maybe you start to make a few tweaks to the love interest himself. But not too many. Just his eye color. Perhaps the clothes he's wearing. Possibly the monologue he delivered to make you swoon . . .

In the previous chapters, we discussed where true love comes from and how to keep your best interests at heart. In this chapter, we'll go over the expectations you should have while you're dating and the qualities you should consider when selecting your ideal mate.

LETTING GO OF "THE ONE"

We've all thought about him over the years. He's made cameos in our dreams, perhaps even earning mentions in our prayers. You may know him as Thor (or Chris Hemsworth). Or maybe his name is Prince Charming. Or Boaz. Whoever this man is for you, I'm sure he shares a common nickname: "Soulmate," "Your perfect match," or "Mr. Right."

It's lovely to entertain the idea of this person, who loves you and dotes on you and complements you in every which way. We've all been there. But it bears repeating: That guy does not exist. Sure, okay, Chris Hemsworth is an actual person, but it's highly unlikely that he will become your soulmate (in fact, he's already married). In reality, there is no such thing as a "perfect man."

Nor is there such thing as a "perfect man" in the Bible (unless, of course, you're referring to the one exception—that is, Jesus—but I digress). It states that "No one is righteous—not even one" (Romans 3:10). In other words, everyone has their faults. Though this may seem like a downer, it's actually great news! The reason being: You are not perfect, either. Although a man will never be "perfect" in every way, pay attention to the attributes that make him uniquely perfect *for you*. Beware of shutting down an opportunity to get to know a really great guy simply because of a few minor flaws. Who knows? His strengths may complement your weaknesses just right.

In modern Christianity, we often use the phrase, "waiting for my Boaz." But even this way of thinking gives us a false impression of what we must do. Ruth never "waited" for Boaz. In fact, she wasn't looking for him at all! Check out what she actually did:

> One day Ruth the Moabite said to Naomi, "Let me go out into the harvest fields to pick up the stalks of grain left behind by anyone who is kind enough to let me do it." Naomi replied, "All right, my daughter, go ahead." So Ruth went out to gather grain behind the harvesters. And as it happened, she found herself working in a field that belonged to Boaz, the relative of her father-in-law, Elimelech (Ruth 2:2–3).

Ruth was attempting to work in the fields so that she could gather food for herself and her mother-in-law, Naomi. She valued her family and prioritized her goals to take care of them. Ruth was not longing for a "perfect man" to come and take care of her. Rather, she stayed true to her values while remaining open to new experiences.

As it happened, she found herself in Boaz's field. This is how Boaz noticed her. Like Ruth, you have to be willing to rid yourself of the mindset that there is a perfect man out there for whom you must intentionally wait. Recall what we covered in chapter 2: Keep an open heart and entertain a willingness to be surprised. By establishing your values and living your life in a way that is conducive to trying new things, visiting new places, and meeting new people, it's possible that you, too, can meet an imperfect man like Boaz!

What's the Word?

*For everything there is a season, a
time for every activity under heaven.*
ECCLESIASTES 3:1

Timing is everything, especially in dating. If the timing isn't right, it doesn't matter how ready you think you are to find "the one."

This factor is frustrating, to be sure. It's outside of your control. But you have the power to choose the values you uphold and the mindset you create and accept that the man you're meant to be with may not in fact align with your long-held idea of Mr. Right.

Try not to force the timing of romance. God's timeline is already set. What you opt to do in an effort to expedite God's plans may not yield desirable results. For example, if you're dating someone you really like, you may decide to take your relationship to the next level without taking the time you need to fully get to know him first. Cracks in his immaculate façade may begin to show. Had you not rushed things, you might've been prepared to handle these issues or avoid them entirely.

The lesson here is to remain patient and steadfast in your faith. If you trust God to put the right people in your life, *at the right time*, you will end up with something truly beautiful.

PINPOINT YOUR DEAL BREAKERS

Of course, you can't accept dates from just anyone! While it's important to go into dating with an open mind, you also have to be discerning. And as kind as you may be, you're simply not going to be attracted to everyone.

Just like you, each potential suitor carries a unique set of traits and characteristics. The question becomes: Which traits and characteristics are you most drawn to? And equally important: Which traits and characteristics can you not stand?

Below, you'll find a handful of traits you might want your mate to have.

How important is it that he . . .

Believes in God? How critical is it for the man you date to have a belief that God exists and plays a role in his life?

Lives out a Christian lifestyle? Does the guy you date have to attend church regularly? Does he need to celebrate Christian holidays? Does he have to have a prayer life? Does he need to have a strong, personal relationship with God?

Has a steady, promising job? Does the man you have a relationship with have to have a steady job? How flexible are you in terms of what kind of job or career he has? Would you be comfortable if he worked long hours, on weekends, or on holidays?

Has an education? Does the guy you're attracted to need to have a certain level of formal education? Would it matter to you if he didn't go to college? Or if he never received a high school diploma?

Has a relationship with his family? Does it matter to you how well the guy you date treats his mother and other women in his family? Conversely, is it okay if he's a "momma's boy"? How open are you to a man for whom spending a lot of time with his family is a big priority?

Is outgoing? Does it matter to you if the man you date is outgoing and socializes well with others? Would it bore you if a man had no desire to explore new places and try new things? Generally, are you looking for more of an introvert or extrovert?

Stays physically fit? How important is a man's physical fitness? Does it matter to you if he exercises regularly? Does he need to practice healthy eating habits?

Treats others in accordance with the Bible? Should the man you date love others in a way that reflects the love described in the Bible? When the Bible talks about the characteristics of love, it states, "Love is patient and kind. Love is not jealous or boastful or proud or rude. It does not demand its own way. It is not irritable, and it keeps no record of being wronged. It does not rejoice about injustice but rejoices whenever the truth wins out. Love never gives up, never loses faith, is always hopeful, and endures through every circumstance" (1 Corinthians 13:4–7). Are you willing to compromise on any of these qualities?

Be within a certain age range? It's often said that age is just a number, but does that hold true for you? Does it matter to you if the man you date is significantly older or younger than you?

Does or does not drink alcohol? Would you date someone who drinks socially? How much drinking is too much? Would you prefer someone who does not drink at all?

Has saved himself for marriage? Are you comfortable dating a man who has had sex in previous relationships? Would it matter to you if he was open to having sex before marriage? Or do you need to date a man who is willing to wait until marriage to have sex?

Wants kids? Should the guy you potentially date want to have kids? What if he already has kids—is that something you'd be open to?

Now that you've reviewed this, try to pinpoint the "deal breakers"—the traits (or lack thereof) that would be grounds for a suitor's immediate disqualification. Likewise, consider the traits with which you might be more flexible or patient. For example, if you're looking for a man to be outgoing and adventurous but you meet someone who's shy, would you allow space for him to grow? If a man has a part-time job and you only want to date guys with full-time work, could you see yourself dating him because of his potential to someday reach that goal?

When you agree to go on a date, pay close attention to the ways in which a man reveals his characteristics. For example, how does he speak to the waitress at a restaurant? How does he talk about his family and friends? At the same time, pay close attention to what he may not be showing you. When something is visibly bothering him, for example, does he choose to remain silent and closed off? These small signs can alert you to whether you're in the presence of a man with whom it may be worth exploring something long-term—or not.

Ultimately, the qualities you wish to find in a man should complement the values that you have already set for yourself (see chapter 2). Aligning them will build chemistry between the two of you and motivate you to deepen the relationship.

And yet, the small differences between you two can set sparks alight, too. His love for the outdoors may give you a deep appreciation of camping, which you may have never experienced before. Your affinity for the arts, on the other hand, may bring out a side of him that he's never explored. Obviously, no two people are exactly alike, so let your differences serve as a catalyst to try new things, create excitement, and propel your relationship forward.

Of course, with God as your guide, you'll want to be mindful of what He tells you to consider when it comes to selecting a suitable man. The Bible says, "Don't judge by his appearance or height, for I have rejected him. The Lord doesn't see things the way you see them. People judge by outward appearance, but the Lord looks at the heart" (1 Samuel 16:7). In other words, do not forget to pay attention to the condition of a man's heart! Though they may not be as readily apparent as some other character traits, how he loves, how he treats others, and how he leads his life are crucial indicators of who a man really is.

Practical Wisdom: Dating Outside of the Faith

What if you meet someone who crosses everything off your list of ideal traits and characteristics, only to discover that they believe in God—but that it's a different god than you yourself believe in?

If a man has a different religious background than yours, such as Buddhism or Islam, would that serve as a deal breaker for you? And if you're unsure, what's the best way for you to know?

The answer is to reflect on yourself and your values: How do you see your future? Is it grounded in your Christian beliefs with a lifestyle that would honor only your God and practice only your faith? Could you share and respect another's values, even if those values came from a different religion? If you were to have children, how do you see yourself raising them? Would their lifestyle be affected by your faith? Would you be willing to allow them to explore and choose different faiths?

In this context, it's equally important to acknowledge that even a man who considers himself a Christian may practice his faith differently than you do. A Catholic and a Baptist could very well believe in the same God, for example, while observing different traditions and rites. Are you willing to compromise on this?

Or is it important for you to find a man who not only shares the same beliefs but also exercises them the same way as you?

There is no real right or wrong answer here. You and you alone are the only one who can know for sure. How important is it for your shared values to be taught under the light of Christianity? If it means a great deal to you, it's best to express this early on in the relationship so that the person you're dating is clear about your beliefs and the beliefs you're looking for in a husband. This will help you determine whether dating someone of a different faith is a possibility for you.

THE FOG OF ATTRACTION

You know the feeling. When the butterflies start to stir. When colors look more vibrant. When songs sound sweeter. When the man you've just started seeing seems like just about the most handsome and wonderful and flawless man in the world. There's no doubt about it: A physical, chemical attraction to someone is a beautiful thing. Do you think that God created Adam and Eve with the intention of them *not* being attracted to one another? Of course not! Just like them, we, too, were created to feel attraction toward others.

Yet as great as attraction is, it can also lead us astray. The Bible tells us, "Promise me, O women of Jerusalem, not to awaken love until the time is right" (Song of Solomon 8:4). If you've ever wondered why so many people seem oblivious to relationship-related red flags, attraction is likely to blame. Because what you *think* is attraction may actually be *infatuation*—the kind of can't-eat-can't-sleep, middle-school crush that burns out as quickly as it ignites. Alternatively, it may be *lust*—the kind of can't-keep-your-hands-off-each-other sexual desire that people so often mistake for love. Both infatuation and lust are functions of attraction, but they don't always result in sustainable long-term relationships. In fact, they tend to push us in the wrong direction, causing us to make compromises for partners who may not deserve them, excuse their faults, and overstep personal boundaries we wouldn't otherwise cross.

So, when your attraction toward someone starts to blossom, ask yourself: What exactly is drawing me toward this man? Is it all of the qualities and characteristics we discussed earlier in the chapter (see page 43)? Is it the fact that he reminds you of God's love and the love described in the Bible? Or, is it mostly just his pecs and perfectly chiseled jaw?

Hopefully, it's all of those things! Even if you've chosen to save yourself for marriage, maintaining a "pure" relationship goes far beyond what you physically consent to. Be wary of the point where attraction slips into infatuation or lust, leading you away from the elements you desire in a healthy, loving relationship.

At the end of the day, whether you've chosen to remain abstinent or not, true emotional and intellectual compatibility is much rarer and more vital for a success-ful, long-term partnership. The looks that you and any man have today will fade over the course of a lifetime. The friendship, laughter, and love that you share with your one and only never will.

Insights and Affirmations

Insights

- Thinking about the "perfect man" is a thing of the past. Set your sights on someone who complements your values with an appealing set of traits and characteristics of their own.
- Is that guy worth a second date? Figure it out by pinpointing any potential deal breakers during your first interaction.
- Attraction toward someone is normal, acceptable, and essential for a healthy relationship. It's the purely physical aspects of infatuation and lust that you have to be on the lookout for.

Affirmations

- Let God guide you to love. Remember to "think about the things of heaven, not the things of earth" (Colossians 3:2).
- Lust shouldn't be what you're after if you're looking for a meaningful, long-lasting relationship. "Instead, pursue righteous living, faithfulness, love, and peace" (2 Timothy 2:22).

This is my command—be strong and courageous! Do not be afraid or discouraged. For the Lord, your God is with you wherever you go. JOSHUA 1:9

Chapter 4

HOW TO MEET SOMEONE

Some women are thrilled by the idea of dressing up and going out to meet someone new. Others are completely terrified. And between old-fashioned blind dates, social media, and the perpetual wave of new dating apps, it can be difficult to know where to even begin.

Truth be told, dating is hard. But the hardest step might be the first one: the decision to get out there and find someone who has the capacity to change your life. In this chapter, I'll help you take the leap by outlining some practical ways to meet a man who's worth your time.

DATING IN THE DIGITAL AGE

Advances in technology have changed almost every aspect of our daily lives, and that includes dating. In the old days, if you lived in a small town, you likely would've ended up pairing off with someone you went to kindergarten with simply due to proximity and a lack of social (and literal) mobility. Nowadays, with the help of smartphones, the world is literally at our fingertips, connecting us with a myriad of people we never would've met otherwise. On top of that, there are countless online dating sites, apps, and social media platforms, all of which can be used to meet a guy who checks off your unique set of boxes—at least on paper. In fact, the internet is the leading source for people getting involved in romantic relationships. According to eharmony.com, 40 percent of Americans are using the internet to engage in online dating (see "How to Meet Someone Online" on page 67).

As much as these tools can help you expand your horizons (see "The Beauty of Openness" on page 34), they can also shrink your dating pool before you've had the chance to test the waters. A dating profile can provide a sketch of a person, but it certainly won't provide you with the full picture. Consequently, you may pass on someone great or find yourself on dates with men whose appealing surface-level traits belie undesirable values.

The ubiquity of technology has given you (and everyone else) an extra layer to hide behind. Online, people are free to be who they *say* they are without having to *show* who they are through body language, facial expressions, and tone. Conversations that flow so easily over text and email may not translate to face-to-face interactions. And while you may think that you're getting a very serious matter across to someone you're dating via text, how they respond—the timing of their reply, their use (or lack thereof) of emojis, their verbiage—could lead to miscommunication, misunderstandings, and other avoidable conflicts (see page 90 for more on communication).

Like it or not, smartphones have become a crucial part of most people's lives. Their incessant demands for our attention—notifications and pings, ceaseless swiping and scrolling—can distract us from staying present with our partners and even become a kind of social safety net to fall back on when we're nervous about going out to meet someone new.

Yet they can also help cultivate and strengthen bonds with the person you're dating. Texting is great for touching base throughout the day and engaging in quick chitchats, while social media is ideal for building rapport through shared articles, memes, and posts.

Of course, anytime you need to discuss something serious, you'll want to do so in person (if possible). Some things are just better done the old-fashioned way!

WHERE TO MEET PEOPLE IRL

Speaking of old-fashioned ways of connecting, there are still a few classic methods you can use to find a love connection. These tried-and-true dating tactics have worked for generations. But in today's world, with so many of our personal and professional interactions conducted online, many feel that it has become increasingly difficult to meet people in the wild.

So, where do we go to meet new people "in real life"? This question has stumped even the best of us. My advice for you is more or less the same message I've been sharing with you throughout this book: know yourself. By frequenting the spots you enjoy while proactively staying open to new experiences, you dramatically boost your odds of meeting your future partner.

Here are a few good places to start.

The Church

While this may seem like a no-brainer for some, for others, the idea of dating someone from church may not be so appealing. I've heard many women say that the suitable guys within their church walls are few and far between. Perhaps the men in your church aren't your type. Maybe there are some who have even already dated a mutual friend. Though certainly not every woman will meet their man in church, there are still good reasons to treat it as a serious option.

Obviously, you and the men in your church already share some common ground. You share the same religious beliefs and, likely, at least some of the values that spring from them. If you decided to date someone from church, you may already have an established circle of shared friends and mentors, which helps when it comes to seeking support, accountability, and opportunities to deepen your relationship. Plus, if your friends and religious leaders trust and approve of someone, it's more likely you'll trust and approve of them, as well.

When you belong to a congregation, it's only natural for you to make friends with other congregants of a similar age. If you belong to the same church you grew up attending, you may have known some of these guys for quite a while now. Making the transition from friendship to a deeper relationship can be much easier than starting as total strangers because you already share a level of trust and familiarity.

Ultimately, going to services, serving in the same ministry, or attending the same Bible study are great opportunities to meet a guy. And although you may think that all the good guys in church are either taken, nonexistent, or not your type, bear in mind that churches always welcome new members. Keep the faith that God's timing is perfect. If you are open to the idea, God could open the doors of romance for you in His very church.

Friends of Friends

Friends are the best. They are there for you when you need them most. They've seen you at your best and also at your worst. While you may endure challenging relationships at work, with your family, or in your romantic relationships, having friends whom you value and trust makes all the difference in the world. When your family is not around, you become a part of your friends' families. When you face professional obstacles, friends give you the encouragement to succeed. When you're stuck in a dead-end relationship, friends help you

What's the Word?

There are "friends" who destroy each other,
but a real friend sticks closer than
a brother. PROVERBS 18:24

We're only as good as the company we keep. And we're only as happy as the friends we surround ourselves with. True friends can build you up, challenge you to grow and become a better version of yourself, and support you through life's ups and downs. Unlike your family, you have the privilege of selecting your friends. These are the people you have *chosen* to love and who still "stick closer than a brother." This is what makes them so special.

As it says in the Bible, "Two people are better off than one, for they can help each other succeed" (Ecclesiastes 4:9). A friend will push you to become your best. They are there to mourn your losses and celebrate your wins.

When considering who could help you meet a great guy, who better to look to than your own friends? They can be trusted with not just your love life but with your heart in general. And when you cannot see things clearly within that relationship, your friends will be the ones to speak the truth to you in love (Proverbs 27:5–6).

face the reality nobody else will; and if things take a turn for the worse, friends will be the first ones there to help you heal. They're in your corner. They want to see you happy. And they know when they spy someone who could be perfect for you.

A good friend would never set you up with someone whom they believed wasn't right for you. After all, they know your likes, dislikes, what you'd be open to, and what you wouldn't. In fact, they might even know you better than you know yourself.

Friends unintentionally expand your social circle, introducing you to new people who, because they're already friends with your friend, are likely worthy of your time and friendship, as well.

In turn, you can *intentionally* enlist your friends to expand your dating pool. Contrary to an algorithm on a dating website or a matchmaker, there is an element of trust you have in your friends that you can't really find anywhere else. They see the full picture of you, not merely a set of variables and preferences.

If you're open to the idea of having a close friend set you down the path of love, the best thing to do is be up-front and honest about it. Share with them that you are looking for love. Ask them if they know anyone who might be worth dating. Confess your desires and concerns. Ply them for advice. Some friends might jump at the chance to help a dear friend find love; others may not feel comfortable with it, as they may be fearful of jeopardizing the friendship if things don't work out.

So, just remember to be open, honest, and unafraid to ask. Think of it this way: If you would do it for your friend, your friend would likely do it for you. You may be pleasantly surprised to discover who your friends have known all this time!

Communal Places That Interest You

As I mentioned earlier, knowing yourself is the key to understanding exactly where to find someone worth dating. The pool of potential partners in a place that interests you is far wider than one that doesn't. If your friends insist on dragging you to the newest nightclub but you have little interest in partying, the chances of running into a guy with similar preferences are slim to none.

Instead, trust your gut. Frequent the places where you feel most at home and seek out new places that pique your curiosity. The goal is not to go to these places with the express intention of meeting someone new; rather, it is to put yourself in situations where you feel most like yourself or are doing things you're passionate about. Not only will this make you more appealing to potential partners, it also puts you in a position to talk to them about things you're both interested in.

Here are a few ideas.

TAKE STOCK OF YOUR FAVORITE HANGOUT

Is there a place where you like to go to relax, unwind, read a book, grab a coffee or cocktail, get some work done, or simply lounge around? Think of a place away from home where you can be yourself.

How to take the next step: If you notice that someone is always at your favorite food spot, a casual smile and eye contact can be all you need to shift gears from sitting alone to sitting with someone new. You can approach someone who seems interested with a casual, "Do you mind if I sit here?" A simple question can lead you into a conversation about any number of things: your taste in food or drink, what brought you to that particular coffeehouse or restaurant, or, if you're alone, what you normally do while enjoying a meal or drink.

JOIN A CLUB

Book club, running club, cooking club, Spanish club—there are so many clubs to choose from! And any club that brings like-minded people together to nurture their interests is a great place to meet a potential mate. You can find these clubs through friends or coworkers with similar interests or at your local library, university, church, Facebook groups, and websites like meetup.com.

How to take the next step: Joining a club can make you feel like the new girl in town. Friendships may already be established, so you'll have to feel your way in. If you notice a guy who is taking a particular interest in you, be open to hearing more about the club's background. Ask him what he enjoys about it, and if the conversation is flowing, perhaps see if he'd be willing to discuss the subject further over a drink or cup of coffee afterward.

ENROLL IN A CLASS

In the same vein as joining a club, there are numerous options to choose from here. The main difference between joining a club and taking a class is that almost everyone taking a class will be new to the group, whereas in a club, there may already be some established friendships.

How to take the next step: Because everyone is likely new to the class, you can strike up a conversation with a guy you're eyeing by simply talking about what you learned in that day's lesson. If the two of you get along, try to become study partners! Studying together for an upcoming quiz or test or working together on a project doesn't come with the same expectations as a date, but it can provide a great opportunity for you to get to know each other outside of class.

TRY THE GYM, FITNESS CLUB, OR YOGA STUDIO

Do you like to work out? Or golf? Or do yoga in the park? These are all great opportunities to nurture self-love in a social setting.

How to take the next step: If you meet someone you're interested in, casually suggest doing something related to the activity on your own terms. For example, if you meet someone at your gym, ask if they're interested in taking a particular class with you there. Perhaps you notice that their method of working out is similar to yours (e.g., you're both swimmers); using this information to ask some general questions about the activity can turn into a personal introduction and maybe more.

PARTICIPATE IN CULTURAL EVENTS

Like music? Go to a concert. Love movies? Attend a local film festival. All about farm life? Visit the county fair. Have a good time while staying open to a fortuitous encounter.

How to take the next step: Typically, these events aren't enjoyed alone. Chances are, you are attending them with other friends. Keep an eye out for opportunities to break free from your friends and strike up a conversation with someone new about the event. While standing in line behind someone, maybe you happen to mention that you love the song that is playing or that you're a fan of the director of the film you're about to see. Think of these small statements as seeds that could blossom into something more: a flirtatious interaction, a casual acquaintance, a friendship, or a relationship. If the conversation is going well, ask him if he'd be interested in a similar event (or the next event in a series). If you're not comfortable going alone, you can make it a group outing and set a date for your friends to meet up with him and his friends.

VOLUNTEER FOR A CHARITABLE ORGANIZATION

Volunteering for a cause you're passionate about is a rewarding activity, regardless of whether or not you meet someone new! But if you happen to strike up a conversation with an attractive guy, you'll have the luxury of knowing that he, like you, has a servant's heart.

How to take the next step: From personal experience, the longer you volunteer somewhere, the more likely you are to end up chatting with someone you like one-on-one. As you're working or perhaps cleaning up after an event, ask questions about their involvement with the charity—how they got started and whether they serve often. This could lead to volunteering together at a future event or even joining a committee, resulting in more quality time together and the continued support of a cause you both care about.

WHAT TO DO WHEN YOU MEET SOMEONE

You're out there minding your own business, when all of a sudden, *bam*! You're met with this fine-looking specimen of a man! No doubt, your mind starts racing a mile a minute.

He is fiiine! *Who is he? Where did he come from?* And then:

Does he have a girlfriend?

You might get caught up in the moment, which is totally natural. But before you let your thoughts about what could come of this first-sight moment spin out of control, ask yourself these questions: What, specifically, has attracted me to this particular individual? Am I sensing a certain vibe from his direction? Has he even noticed me?

Not only should you check your heart during that initial eye-locking moment, but you should also remember to stay true to yourself! There is absolutely no need to act in a particular way or say something just to impress him. The best impression you can make is the one that displays the real you!

Oftentimes, names aren't thrown out there until you've established some sort of connection—with a smile, a laugh, or an exchange that makes you want to learn more about each other. So, if your first words to each other aren't, "Hi, my name is _____", it doesn't mean that you won't trade names (and maybe even numbers) later on.

The one connection you and he will instantly share—other than chemistry—is the environment in which you meet. Use this to your advantage. Talk about where you are. Even asking, "What brings you here?" is enough to jumpstart a conversation.

As the two of you make light conversation, pay attention to where his eyes go. If those bad boys keep dropping down to check on your good girls, then he might be talking to you just to get somewhere else. But if he's smiling, the eye contact is there, his body is leaning in, and he's giving you all of his attention, you may just have someone on your hands who deserves to know your name.

Once you meet someone who's giving you this kind of attention, it's important to keep in mind the sights you set during the previous chapter (see page 40). No matter how cute he is or how much he makes you laugh, this new guy will never fit your mold of "the one." And just because you have caught his eye doesn't mean that you have to sacrifice your values and interests. Remember, being yourself and exhibiting the traits that make you unique are part of your appeal! If this guy can't see that, it's his loss.

If you're feeling into someone, and you feel that he is really into you, too, be open to the prospect of further conversations, even a date. But also, be mindful of the

Practical Wisdom: Pivoting to the Date

You're talking to a guy and the conversation is flowing. As you're chatting, you think to yourself: *How great would it be if the two of us went out on a date?* But how, exactly, do you pivot the conversation in that direction?

If the conversation is going smoothly, chances are the guy is looking for a seamless way to ease into that topic, as well. However, some guys are wary of coming off as overly aggressive; others may simply be scared to put themselves out there; others still may take things slower than you'd like because they think it's the respectful thing to do (oftentimes, it is!).

Gauge where the conversation is going and where you can lead it by bringing up future events that could serve as opportunities to meet up. Depending on where you are, use the location as common ground to reconnect. If you're at the gym, for example, you could mention a class that's going on there next week and casually ask if he'd like to go. Alternatively, see if he takes a hint and offers to meet with you first. If your location is not the best place in the world to reconnect (like, if you're talking in line at the grocery store), then be open to using a simple yet confident phrase, such as, "This was nice. We should meet again sometime." See where those bold words can take you!

fact that he may never call you. If that's the case, it's likely due to circumstances outside of your control.

No matter what, enjoy the interaction for what it is: a really great moment with a really great guy. Sooner or later, you're bound to have a conversation with someone who wants nothing more than to have another conversation with you. Don't be afraid to open up and put yourself out there—the more interactions you have, the greater your odds of meeting someone you'll want to get to know better.

HOW TO MEET SOMEONE ONLINE

Online dating: Some love it, some hate it. Be that as it may, it is a viable form of dating, and if you are looking for a place to start, going online could be a great opportunity for you—even if it turns out to be just as complicated and challenging as dating in the real world.

Do I know people who met their spouses on apps or dating sites? Absolutely. Have I also heard horror stories? You bet. The real question is: Are you open to exploring this new dating venture and seeing where things go?

Online dating can feel uncomfortable at first. After all, you are interacting with complete strangers. Some people believe that making a connection with someone virtually is purely based on physical appearances; in truth, there's always the possibility that the person you meet online will not take you seriously in real life. He may even "ghost" you—disappear without a trace—if he decides to enter into an exclusive relationship with someone else. All this can make online dating seem daunting. But the reality is, the circumstances are not so different when you meet someone the "old-fashioned" way, either. According to a 2019 study from the Pew Research Center, more than half of Americans (54 percent) say relationships that begin on a dating app are just as successful as those that begin in person.

Plus, as I mentioned earlier in this chapter, online dating can vastly expand your dating pool. You could even meet someone on the other side of the world and fall in love! I have personally seen this happen. Dating online will also push you out of your comfort zone. And if you're struggling to get past the stigma surrounding online dating, let me reiterate: *Many people have gotten and continue to get married to people they meet online.*

What follows is a representative sample of online dating platforms you might want to look into, along with their biggest pros and cons.

Christian Mingle

Pros: Everyone on this site has openly claimed that they are Christians, which removes the guesswork in terms of where they stand with their faith. Additionally, this site constitutes one of the largest dating pools for Christians, so you'll have plenty of options if you're looking to get serious with someone.

Cons: Because of sheer size, it may be overwhelming to meet so many potential dates in one setting. And while the paid subscription gets you all of the bells and whistles, the free version comes with some limitations.

Bumble

Pros: This is a swipe-based app where, once two people match (i.e., when both swipe in the direction that indicates interest), the woman must initiate the conversation. Since the onus is on you, men tend to be pretty honest in their profiles. And since you have the control, you can take the connection as deep as you desire. Whether that's looking for something casual or a more serious relationship—it's up to you!

Cons: Unfortunately, guys who lie or are disrespectful can be found almost everywhere (to their credit, Bumble has historically been very good at handling instances where users have reported someone getting out of line). Because the app gives women the power to make the first move, it requires you to step up and be assertive in order to make connections. So, if you shy away from this sort of approach, this might not be the app for you.

Coffee Meets Bagel

Pros: Although it may be a little less popular than other mainstream dating sites, this one may be beneficial for starting out. Like Hinge (another popular dating app), Coffee Meets Bagel uses your social circle to yield a limited number of ostensibly higher-quality matches every day at noon. This app won't feel so overwhelming, and you'll be able to consider your choices more easily (and seriously). Although men on the app can choose to like, swipe, or "priority like," women can also take it a step further and start the conversation!

Cons: Because of its smaller dating pool, you may not find a match right away, which could give you the false impression that the app isn't working or that there aren't any good guys using it.

eharmony

Pros: It's one of the oldest and most popular online dating services out there, and with that kind of credibility, it's no wonder men and women continue to come back to this dating site. This site is for those who intend to find a serious match. Used by people of all ages, faith backgrounds, and more, the world is your oyster on this site. While the sign-up process is relatively time-consuming, it's intended to help you find a good match. And with a track record of connecting couples every 14 minutes, it is definitely worth checking out!

Cons: It can feel stuffy and overwhelming to meet so many people at once. Men can immediately message you if they are interested, so you could potentially receive a lot of messages from guys that you have no interest in. With regards to the sign-up process, there may be some questions that pigeonhole you into a response that is not entirely accurate. For example, if someone answers that they aren't religious, the questionnaire will continue to ask questions about church, forcing them to respond in a way that implies they do go to church. It can be confusing at times to try to respond to all of the questions honestly, especially when you've already indicated on your profile that some topics don't apply.

Our Time

Pros: This is an online dating service for daters exclusively over the age of 50, so if you are searching for a partner in this age range, this is the place for you!
Cons: This site is designed to solely address the interests and needs of those who fit in this demographic. So, if you're open to a wider age range or looking to meet men who are younger, you may want to look elsewhere.

Social Media

Pros: With a new online dating site or app popping up every minute, it can be hard to know which one is worth your time. If you feel overwhelmed, you can always turn to your social media platforms and send someone you know (or a friend of a friend) a direct message. Like dating apps, there will be a social media platform that fits your unique needs, comforts, and interests. Facebook offers the opportunity to reach out to people through your connections with family and past friends (such as your old high school classmates). Instagram allows you to express yourself visually and is a nonthreatening way to connect with people you've just met or want to get to know better. Snapchat, with its ephemeral video messages, is fun, friendly, flirty, and attracts a younger population. TikTok is all about making fun videos to laugh and connect over. Each of these platforms allows you to privately message another user if you decide to pursue a connection—and break the ice with a funny meme, relevant post, or conversation starter about a mutual friend or interest.

Cons: Because the primary objective of social media is not romantic, you aren't going to be able to tailor your dating pool beyond sharing your relationship status (something that can only be done on Facebook). Furthermore, the amount of space you're given to describe yourself varies from platform to platform, and unless you actively search for someone beyond your established following, you won't meet anyone outside of your own circle. If you're looking expand your horizons, you'll have to take a further step to engage in Facebook groups, comment on other users' Instagram posts, or search for topics of interest using hashtags and the like.

BUILDING AND EVALUATING AN ONLINE DATING PROFILE

When it comes to creating an online dating profile, the best thing you can do is be honest. Clearly lay out your intentions in your profile's description section and stick to your standards once you meet someone. When sharing personal information about yourself, consider what you would share on your first date. If what you've included is too personal to be shared on an actual date, then you may want to remove it from your profile. For example, you wouldn't reveal your most embarrassing moment or how your last relationship ended with someone you just met, would you? The same criteria should apply to the details you share on your profile.

Though it differs from site to site (and app to app), you can use the profile space you're provided to share personal facts about yourself (what you do for a living, what your hobbies are, and the like). But it's also where you can describe, in some detail, what you're expecting to find in the online dating world. However, be aware that sharing the traits you are looking for in a man could be hit-or-miss—men could claim to possess all the traits you're looking for just to connect with you. Pretending to be someone you're not is easy when you're online because there is no way to know the truth beyond what you each choose to share until you actually meet and spend time getting to know one another. For this reason, stick to sharing your values, your expectations, and your idea of a fun date—whether that's going to a movie, a new exhibit at a local museum, or taking a trip to a nearby farmers' market. Finally, have a close friend read over your profile description to confirm that what you've written sounds genuine. How much you get out of a dating site depends on the effort and truthfulness you put into it.

As for the photos, include at least three distinct photos of yourself: one that is fairly recent and very cute, one full-body photo that is somewhat older, and one that is somewhat less flattering (perhaps a candid shot that was not taken on your best day ever). Together, these three pictures should cover all of the bases of how you look. They'll give whoever sees your profile an honest depiction of what you look like—what you *really* look like—and an idea of what to expect if they choose to start a conversation.

When evaluating someone else's profile, be on the lookout for red flags. If a profile emphatically highlights the man's physical features—for example, a series of vain shirtless photos—it's likely a reflection of surface-level desires. If a profile is excessively wink-wink flirtatious, it's a strong indicator that the man who created it is looking for something casual. If a profile is too vague or doesn't provide enough basic personal information, it's a telltale sign that this guy is not a genuine person and does not have a genuine interest in meeting someone new.

On the other hand, if you notice a profile of a man who is genuinely good-looking, both in a more casual photo and a photo in which he's smiling, it may prompt you to stop and take a closer look. Perhaps his profile seems down-to-earth and what he's written makes you laugh. Now, if he's included that he is looking for a relationship, without the extra smooth-talking fluff or canned lines that make it seem disingenuous, you might have a potential winner! Keep in mind, when you check out someone's profile, that you want to feel as though it would be easy to get to know him—or as if you've already known him for years. Oftentimes, this hunch will be confirmed (or invalidated) within the first batch of messages you exchange.

THE SEVEN COMMANDMENTS OF ONLINE DATING

Before you leave for your first date with someone you've met online, it's important to set some basic safety rules for yourself. After all, the person you're meeting is still technically a complete stranger.

1. **Talk to the guy several times before you agree to meet in person.** You can text, call, or set up a video chat to get to know him before you agree to meet up in real life.

2. **Set a date that takes place during daylight hours.** This helps you avoid any late-night activities with which you may be uncomfortable. There are lots of activities that you can do during the daytime (such as going to brunch or coffee) that could then turn into something else (like a museum visit or walk in the park), so think of this limitation as an opportunity rather than a disadvantage.

3. **Meet in a public place.** Pick a meeting place in public so that you will be safe from anything that could potentially happen behind closed doors.

4. **Drive to the date by yourself or take public transportation.** If the date goes south, this will prevent your date from knowing your home address. In the unlikely circumstance your car won't start or your public transportation is no longer running once you're done with your date, call an Uber, a taxi, or a friend to come pick you up. If for some reason your date must be your ride, have him drop you off at a public location (such as a store or coffee shop) that is a safe walking distance from your home rather than your actual address. Having a friend meet you at that public location can add an extra measure of safety to the scenario. Also, there should be no need to lie or fabricate the reason as to why you

are choosing to keep him away from your home. It's okay to be straightforward with your date, letting him know that you simply do not want him to know where you live until trust is built.

5. **Check in with a friend after 15 minutes.** Tell a friend where you're going and who you'll be with. Once the date has started, text your friend and let them know that you are doing well, or, if you're not, that you need some assistance. If it's the latter, a simple text reading "call" is an easy way to let your friend know that you need them to call you and give you a safe excuse to make an exit before the date goes any further.

6. **Do not share too much personal information up front.** After seeing each other's dating profiles, you should have plenty to talk about while on your first date. Use your time together to elaborate on the details you've shared in your profile and leave the more personal topics for if and when you feel he can be trusted.

7. **Stay sober.** While having a drink or two may be fine, depending on your tolerance, drinking too much on a date with someone you've just met can lead to unwise—not to mention, unsafe—choices.

Insights and Affirmations

Insights

- Online dating can be intimidating, but be open to the possibility of using it to meet someone new and interesting.
- As long as you are aware of yourself and what you enjoy doing, you should be able to step out of your comfort zone and go places where you could potentially meet someone who shares the same interests as you.
- Men do not always have to make the first move! If you find that a conversation is going well or an online profile piques your interest, don't be afraid to strike up a conversation.

Affirmations

- No matter what situation you place yourself in to meet someone new, you should always be mindful of guarding your heart (see Proverbs 4:23).
- Honesty is key. Use it to find the right person in the right setting and remember to be truthful when describing who you are and what you hope to gain from dating (see Proverbs 24:26).

Three things will last forever—faith, hope, and love—and the greatest of these is love. 1 CORINTHIANS 13:13

Chapter 5

THE ROAD TO COUPLEDOM

As rewarding, fun, and exciting (or occasionally terrifying) as dating can be, it's simply an imperfect means to a more perfect end. The Bible tells us "faith, hope, and love" will last forever. Although you may experience plenty of "faith" and "hope" as you date, when all is said and done, it's the "love" you're really after.

Going on dates is the first step toward finding someone who's worth the time and investment a relationship requires. But what steps must you take to go from dating someone to being in an exclusive relationship with them? In this chapter, we'll discuss the delicate transition to coupledom, starting with the first date.

THE FIRST DATE

So, you've managed to score a first date with a guy you're interested in (or, perhaps, a guy your friends *hope* you'll be interested in). You have plans to meet at a restaurant, or a café, or the park tomorrow afternoon, but for today, the thrilling prospect of what *could* be is distracting you from what's yet to be done—the date itself!

First dates are acts of bravery. And that bravery stands to be rewarded with a really nice guy who has the potential to become a really nice husband. Nerves are natural, physiological indicators of both excitement (for the date) and alertness (in the event it goes sideways). Maybe it's been a while since your last first date; maybe it's your very *first* first date ever. Things, of course, may not work out as you hope. Worse, the date could get canceled. With so many outcomes to consider, it's important to take baby steps here. Instead of luxuriating in this flood of new feelings, let's talk about what you can do to ready yourself for a successful date.

As much as you prepare for this interaction outwardly—through the outfit you choose or the way you style your hair—it's also necessary to prepare inwardly. Confidence is key, but you can only convey confidence when you feel a sense of inner peace and assurance that you are doing everything you can to produce a good outcome.

Let God be your guide and keep the following dating tips in mind when going out with someone new.

Pray About It

What can prayer do for your first date? Well, where do I begin? For starters, prayer is a dialogue you have with God that helps bring you closer to His love.

In praying about your first date, avoid simply praying that things go well. Instead, pray about your emotions—whether you are feeling nervous, excited, or scared—and for your safety before, during, and after the date. Use prayer as a way to reflect on your boundaries and ask God to help you remain aware of them throughout the date.

Praying before your first date is a great way to share what's in your heart with God. The Bible tells us to, "Come close to God, and God will come close to you" (James 4:8). Drawing close to God through prayer will keep Him on your mind as you carry on your first date, giving you a sense of peace, reassurance, and clarity.

Naturally, you can pray to Him as much as you want, so start praying over your first date the minute it's set! You can pray out loud, journal your thoughts, or even ask a close friend to pray with you as you prepare for your date.

Get in the Right Mindset

It's not uncommon to experience some bad vibes in the days leading up to a first date. Maybe you feel like you're wasting your time; maybe you feel like no matter what you wear, you just aren't pretty enough—or deserving enough—to date someone worthwhile. This is normal. Yet it's critical that you do not let such negative thoughts (lies!) prevent you from seeing this date as an opportunity filled with hope.

The truth is, dating is just a stop on the road to marriage; it's not worth dwelling on all the negative things that *could* happen. You *are* worthy of meeting someone who aligns with your values and complements your unique characteristics. Sure, bad things can happen on a first date. But what if something *really* good happens instead? Ultimately, the fear of a date going poorly shouldn't overshadow the prospect of it going well; the majority of bad dates are minor inconveniences compared to the life-changing ramifications of one great date.

As you prepare, focus on the beauty behind this concept: Your first date should be a mutually enjoyable experience where God's love is shared, whether marriage eventually happens or not. Who you are and how you look should be accepted by *you*—that's what really matters. Internalizing these truths and taking an optimistic approach to the date will bring out the confidence you need to be your best self and have a nice time.

Don't Be Afraid to Take an Active Role in the Conversation

Please, ladies: Do not go on a date expecting the man to do all of the talking.

Now, if you're shy, I get it. It can be really difficult to place yourself outside of your comfort zone and engage in conversation with someone new. But the entire point of going on a first date is to get to know the other person better. While actions are great, in this case, words are going to mean everything.

As you prepare for your first date, be sure to keep a few topics in mind that you might like to discuss. Although you may think that the conversation will blossom out of nowhere (and sometimes it does!), it's best to be prepared in the event it does not.

A few go-to topics might include: current events (though you may want to refrain from the political chat); how the date came about (did you meet through a mutual friend? A dating app?); what you enjoy doing for fun; what your present workweek looks like; your favorite music, movies, or TV shows; or the ever-reliable discussion of whatever is happening in your immediate surroundings. Did you just see a movie? Talk about what you liked or didn't like about it. Are you grabbing a coffee? Tell him your coffee-related preferences. Going out for dinner? Parse the menu out loud, share your favorite foods, discuss the ambiance or background music, and so on.

And if conversation in the shallow end is going well, don't be afraid to dive into deeper waters. If your date asks you about your family, your faith, or your opinion when it comes to a touchy subject, be honest! Take advantage of the opportunity to express your true thoughts and measure your date's responses against your values. Provided that you always speak with love and respect, it's okay to agree to disagree on some things; you don't want to say you agree with your date on a point you don't really believe in, simply to please him. Just be yourself and be kind.

Don't Neglect Your Past

I would not recommend bringing up your past relationship(s) on a first date, because it can result in you revealing raw emotions to someone who doesn't care about the guy who came before him. However, as you prepare for this date, keep in mind what's happened in the past.

Simply put, the past—all the reasons why things didn't work out before—will remind you of what you do (and don't) want in the future. Recall the red flags from your previous relationship(s); if you spot any on this first date, you'll know it's not worth your time to go on a second.

Past relationships can also remind you of things you wish you'd done differently. So, think of a first date as a fresh start. History does not have to repeat itself; take the lessons that you have learned from the past and apply them to the present. And remember: Not all men are the same! Using your pain to protect yourself from future hurt can prevent you from getting to know someone great. While it's important to honor the lessons you've learned from previous relationships, keep an open mind and give this new guy a chance to start off with a clean slate.

Trust Your Gut

As the date goes on, you'll likely start to experience all sorts of thoughts and feelings. It may be overwhelming. You may find yourself questioning everything you do and say. You may find yourself questioning everything your date does and says. That's just how us girls are wired! If you're like me, at least, you tend to overthink things.

When this happens, it can be difficult to decipher which of your feelings are real and worth putting into action; desire has the power to distort, molding the man in front of you to look and sound more like the man you want him to be. Because of this, it's wise to continue to pray for the clarity you need. But it's also prudent to trust your gut. Your instincts are your instincts for a reason—they're your first line of defense for evaluating a potential mate.

If something doesn't feel right on your date, do not ignore it. Being in a place that makes you uncomfortable should encourage you to remove yourself from a potentially harmful situation, whether that means simply changing the subject, saying "no" to something you're not ready for, or walking away from the date altogether. Do not be willing to do whatever your date wants at the expense of your own peace and comfort. As long as you are holding onto the peace God is giving you, then your heart will be guarded and you can move toward a relationship that will bring you the happiness you deserve (see Philippians 4:7).

On the other hand, you should also trust your gut when things are going right! If you are genuinely having a blast on your date and don't want it to end, try not to second-guess yourself. If you are prompted to step out of your comfort zone and are feeling a sense of peace about it, go for it!

DO YOU WANT TO SEE HIM AGAIN?

After every first date, you're left with the all-important question: Do you want to see him again?

Consider this question seriously and be mindful not to answer "yes" for the wrong reasons. You may feel obligated to go on a second date because you do not wish to offend someone. Or, the pressure to agree to more dates could be motivated by your own fears—that there are no other good guys out there or that this is your best available option. Maybe the guy was so adamant about his desire to see you again that you feel as though you've embraced an affirmative answer without having a chance to really think it over.

Regardless of what the man wants, this is exclusively your decision. Let me repeat: It does not matter how your answer will affect the guy; what you choose to do after your first date is your choice and no one else's. Trust your gut, trust in God, consider what went right, and consider what went wrong. Reflect on your values and the qualities you're looking for in a man. If everything is aligned, then by all means, see him again! Even if you're just going off a spark, give that feeling a chance to flourish, if only for one more date.

In any event, be confident in your decision. Although it may be difficult for you to reject someone, understand that someone better *will* come along, and know that putting your own needs and wants first will always yield a better outcome.

So . . . what is it going to be?

If You Do Want to See Him Again . . .

What exciting news! If you are into a guy who took you on a date and you would like to see him again, make sure he knows. If he asks you to go on a second date, do not hesitate to say "yes." The game of "making a man wait" or "playing hard to get" is just that: a game. Men like women who know what they want. If you're sure you want to see him again, let him know up front.

If this conversation didn't transpire during the first date, it's perfectly okay to express to him—via text, a phone call, or the next time you see him in a non-date setting—that you had a great time and would love to do something again soon. Taking the lead in this discussion doesn't have to feel pushy or aggressive. Letting him know you enjoyed the date and would like to spend more time together allows you to be assertive, without placing undue pressure on him to make a decision.

Here's an example of what this might look like:

"Hey! I had a really great time with you the other day! [Mention something you liked about the date] and I'd love to do it again soon!"

If you hear back, great! Proceed to get to know him better. But don't try to manipulate the situation. You wouldn't like it if a man continued to bring up a second date as a way to pressure you into it, and those same standards apply to you. Simply by expressing your interest, you are being open and direct in letting him know what you want. It's up to him to decide if the feelings are mutual.

Sorry to hear things didn't work out so well! This is quite all right. Ultimately, knowing a second date isn't worth your time is a good thing. Give yourself some credit for saying "yes" to the first date, venturing outside of your comfort zone, and expanding your horizons. Take what you learned from the experience and apply it to the next one.

But make sure you tie up loose ends first. Just because you've decided not to see this guy again, doesn't mean you shouldn't treat him with respect. If he was cordial and you simply aren't interested, it's best to be clear and forthright about your choice. You don't want to lead him on—the more you equivocate, cloaking your rejection in abstract terms, the more likely he is to think that he still has a chance with you. With kindness, grace, and clarity, let your date down easy. If you'd still like to be friends, tell him as much; if you weren't friends to begin with, explain that while you had a nice time, you don't wish to date him anymore.

The text you send can be as simple and straightforward as this:

"Hey! It was great meeting you, but I don't think we're a good fit for each other. Best of luck to you!"

Naturally, after receiving a message like that, he may have some follow-up questions. He might want to know what went wrong or which factors resulted in your decision. If you feel the need to explain your reasoning, be polite but brief. Don't critique his character for not meeting your expectations. The point of this conversation is to establish closure. God teaches us to speak and act with love, and this letdown should be handled no differently. If he chooses not to reply after receiving your message, let it go and move on.

If your date was overtly rude or left you feeling uncomfortable, however, immediately cut all ties. If he contacts you, let him know that you're not a good match and won't be going on future dates. Should he persist, don't feel the need to respond to his texts or calls; "ghost" him, if need be.

Remember, there's no need to feel bad about letting a man down if you believe you're making the best choice for you.

What's the Word?

The tongue can bring death or life; those who love to talk will reap the consequences. PROVERBS 18:21

Rejection is not an easy thing to feel. Nor is it an easy thing to deal out. And when it comes to dating, particularly first dates, rejection can feel awkward—like an unnecessary confrontation. Understandably, many people do their best to justify their aversion to rejecting someone directly, opting to "ghost" them instead. Ultimately, it's much harder to let someone down than to run away from letting them down altogether.

Yet "ghosting" can be selfish. And, as God teaches, rejection can be handled with respect, honesty, and tact. The Bible says there is power in the tongue: the ability to "bring death or life" to any situation. Instead of letting someone down with accusations or judgments, simply let him know that you had a nice time but don't see things working out. You can leave it at that, lest you risk "reap[ing] the consequences"; when it comes to rejection, being concise can prevent you from unintentionally hurting someone's feelings. But if you must say more, bring life into the situation by affirming his virtues (i.e., "You're such a considerate guy!"), and point out that *he* is not the issue—the issue is merely the connection between the two of you.

GOOD DATERS ARE BETTER COMMUNICATORS

The best couples rely on effective communication. Without it, your relationship won't stand a chance. On the contrary, if you make a concerted effort from the get-go and continue to work on communication every step of the way, there's no telling how far you two can go!

There are many ways to get a message across, and no two people communicate in exactly the same way. You may be more forthcoming and trusting by nature, for example, whereas your partner may be more withholding and calculating. As a result, you may think you're communicating clearly, even when you're not. Thoughts and emotions left unexpressed (or misunderstood) can create major gaps between a new or would-be couple—gaps filled with uncertainty, confusion, and mistrust.

Use God's Word as your guide. The Bible teaches us that speaking in love with patience, honesty, and grace not only strengthens the communication between you and the man you're dating but also fortifies your relationship against the challenges it may face in the future.

When communicating on and between dates, as you follow the winding path to coupledom, consider the following advice.

Lead with Honesty

Think about how it feels to be completely honest with yourself and the person you're with. To hold nothing back. To express your wants and needs. To know that this person accepts you for all your strengths and all your flaws, your values and your idiosyncrasies. Liberating, isn't it? Regardless of how natural or difficult it is for you to be honest with someone you're dating, few virtues are as vital for the long-term health of a relationship.

Honesty plays an influential role in a variety of scenarios both positive and negative, major and minor.

It can shape the pivotal conversation where you finally share how much you *really* like someone. Or, it can form a boundary or value you choose to enforce. If you dislike something about your relationship early on, being honest about it will clear a path for moving forward.

Oftentimes, honesty brings difficult decisions to the fore. You may come to realize, for example, that after a few dates, you no longer feel this man is right for you. Being honest with yourself—and with the man you're dating—will allow you to make the tough decision to part ways. Alternatively, you may notice some red flags waving in the winds of your dates—honoring them with honesty and humility will help you address these issues before they grow worse.

No matter what, honesty will keep you and your values aligned. God is honest, and, therefore, He instructs us to be as well. As the Bible tells us, "We are careful to be honorable before the Lord, but we also want everyone else to see that we are honorable" (2 Corinthians 8:21). Nothing good comes from holding back our honest feelings, thoughts, and opinions in dating and relationships.

Find the Right Communication Style

As I mentioned before, everyone has a different communication style. Moreover, we all respond to these various styles in different ways. Though you may find blunt communicators effective, your partner may find that level of directness abrasive or insulting; where you may find physical touch comforting during difficult conversations, your partner may bristle. The fact is, no matter how you communicate, when you decide to talk to your date about something, they still might only really *hear* a fraction of the message you're trying to get across.

This may have less to do with the clarity of what you're saying and more to do with the misaligned communication styles that you and the man you're dating use—like a puzzle piece that doesn't *quite* fit. Women who do not understand this often feel as though what they are saying isn't important enough to be heard, and this assumption can make women believe that they themselves are not worthy enough of the man they're with. Neither of these things are true!

Part of being in a relationship is learning how to tailor your communication style to fit that of your partner (and vice versa). When you're dating someone new, be open to the idea of adapting to your date's style of communication—provided, of course, that it doesn't establish unhealthy patterns (where, for example, you feel pressured not to say what's on your mind). To determine whether you're operating from a place of mutual understanding, you can always ask the question, "What did you hear me say?" or "Is what I said clear?" This is not meant to be condescending. Make it clear that you're asking solely for the purpose of resolving any differences between the message you sent and the one he received.

Don't be offended if you have to repeat yourself. And don't feel confused if you and your date are still on two completely different pages on a topic, even after you've explained your position clearly. The best way to get on the same wavelength is to listen to each other and be direct about how you would like to communicate. The Bible teaches us that, "Spouting off before listening to the facts is both shameful and foolish" (Proverbs 18:13). Does the man you're dating need to respond to every single thing you say to show you that he's listening? Do you need him to come up with advice every time you voice a concern, or is simply allowing you to vent enough? Understand what you need, then let him know—and listen to what he needs from you in return.

Maintain an Open Dialogue About Your Faith

Your faith may be very important to you, and it might be equally important that the person you choose to date shares this stance. Yet just because you are a Christian dating someone who claims to also believe in God does not necessarily mean that you both have the same degree of faith. Your idea of what a Christian lifestyle looks like may be completely different from someone else's.

How you pray, how often you pray, your style of worship (i.e., what songs you like to listen to, whether you worship in silence or enjoy dancing, etc.), and your personal relationship with God—all of these factors could be different for you and the person you're dating. Not to mention, your views on intimacy: Are you both in agreement about what's acceptable within your relationship and what's not? What are your beliefs on sex before marriage? Do you believe it's acceptable to move in together before marriage? What boundaries should you both be aware of to protect your faith and personal values? Just because you and the man you're dating have some diverging viewpoints doesn't mean either of you is a "bad Christian"; it's simply a reminder that everyone is on their own spiritual journey.

Ultimately, as long as you are both being sincere about your beliefs, there are no right or wrong answers when it comes to your faith. Be sure that you and your date maintain an open conversation about your religious convictions so that there are no mixed feelings or emotions. Though you may find it very easy to pray together, attend church together, or have conversations about your faith, this approach may be new or difficult for the man you're dating. Is that a deal breaker for you? Or do you simply need to talk about it and come to a mutual understanding? Is there any way that you can both learn to love and honor God in your own separate ways, while also respecting each other's faith?

Spend time discussing what is important to you regarding your faith. Don't be afraid to explain or go into detail about why you pray, worship, and believe in the ways that you do. Be open to exploring his methods, as well. Be honest with what you need in this area, what you're willing to compromise on, how you can understand each other's point of view, and (hopefully) where you and your date can learn and grow from each other's faithful insights. Remember, God looks at the condition of the heart, not at what you are doing (or not doing) for the sake of someone else.

Assess Where the Relationship Is (or Is Not) Going

The expectations you have for your relationship should not be a mystery to the person you're dating. Just as you wouldn't get in your car without a destination in mind, every relationship requires a sense of direction, as well as continued communication as to how (and when) you plan to get there.

Many people assume that dating follows a particular route at a certain speed. First, kissing is okay. Then, perhaps, sleeping together becomes normal. Soon after, you're talking every day instead of every other day. But all of these expectations are based on past experiences, and the person you're dating is not a past experience—nor are you a past experience for him. Your relationship together is entirely new, singular; the route you take to coupledom may not feature the same stops as the routes each of you have taken in the past. As such, you'll want to make sure you're addressing your concerns and expectations in the early stages of your relationship and that you're continuing to address them as the relationship progresses.

Bringing up these expectations can be awkward. It may feel as though you are being too demanding at a time when the relationship is "not that serious." Perhaps you feel as though you should already know some of these things, when, in fact, the particulars are quite hazy. For example, after dating someone for more than six months, you may understandably get the impression that he loves you, even though he hasn't actually said it. Maybe, after being in a loving relationship for over a year, you assume he knows you want to get married, even if he has never made it clear those feelings are mutual. No matter how many hints you drop about a particular ring you'd love to receive by Christmas, if you have never told him outright that marriage and a family are what you want, you may be disappointed when you open your gift to find another set of earrings. By not clarifying your desires and concerns, you risk leaving a whole lot up to someone else's interpretation. This can lead to miscommunication and increased pressure to take the relationship in a direction you weren't prepared for it to go.

So, if you are willing to keep seeing someone after the third or fourth date, consider expressing any goals or concerns you may have about the relationship. Perhaps he mentioned that he enjoys a drink or two after a long day of work, but you prefer a lifestyle without alcohol; perhaps he's been a *bit* too touchy-feely with you, and, moving forward, you would like to take things a little slower. Don't be afraid to ask the hard questions. It's better to seek clarity than to go on pretending you know all the answers.

Gauge When to Deepen Your Conversations

The longer you date someone, the more intimate your conversations should become. You wouldn't share your deepest, darkest secrets with a man you just met, would you? Consider the Bible's instructions to "guard your heart" (Proverbs 4:23). If you open your heart too quickly to someone you've yet to get to know and trust, it places you in a vulnerable position and leaves you more exposed to hurt.

On your first date, you and your date should cover the basics (your profession, your interests, and the like) and evaluate whether a relationship is worth exploring. The more dates you go on, the more layers you'll unearth in your conversations. Be patient. You don't want to roll out every loaded conversation within the first few dates. When you barely know each other, it might be too much for him (or you) to handle. But as you grow to like each other, then trust each other, and, later, love each other, gradually take what you talk about to the next level. To start, try introducing open and honest discussions about faith, family, past hardships, and hopes for the future.

By the time you are standing at the altar, looking at the man you are about to marry, you should feel very comfortable and secure talking to him about everything. And I mean everything—heartbreaks, finances, deep fears, sexual preferences, and more. There should be no topic under the sun that you're afraid to talk about with this man.

Here's a possible timetable to help you gauge when it's time to have deeper conversations. Keep in mind, every relationship is different! Don't feel like you have to strictly adhere to this timeline.

During the first month of dating, *you should get to know each other. Discuss what you're looking for in a boyfriend, set your expectations,* and share your values. At this stage, you're still figuring out if a relationship is worth pursuing.

In the first month of being in an exclusive relationship, enforce your values and aim to achieve a deeper understanding of each other's personality, communication style, and boundaries. Make an effort to learn more about his upbringing, career goals, and current setbacks.

From three to six months month of being in an exclusive relationship, you'll want to determine if the relationship is moving forward or if it has become stagnant. Establish your expectations going forward (if you see the relationship progressing), and really get to know each other's inner circles, such as family, friends, and coworkers. Explore what you both like, want, and need in order to cultivate a healthy relationship.

From six months to a year of being in an exclusive relationship, you should feel comfortable enough with your boyfriend that you can speak to him about your needs, concerns, intentions for the future, and current personal struggles (e.g., finances, fears, worries, concerns, etc). Most important, you should both have a clear idea of whether this relationship has a real, long-term future.

Practical Wisdom: When to Have "The Talk"

You've gone on a few dates. Get-to-know-you conversations have given way to flirtatious banter. There's a glimmer in your eye that only he can see, and he has a way of making you smile whenever you're with him, for no reason in particular. You're not sure when, exactly, you knew that you liked him—like, *really* liked him—but you're positive you do.

It seems like your feelings are reciprocated. The two of you are talking a little bit more each day. He tells you he's thinking about you all the time. You've been praying that God would keep the doors open and let this guy be the real deal. So far, so good. All of the right things are happening . . . this could be it.

On social media, it's obvious that you both have a thing for each other. He likes your posts and you leave comments on his. There's even a selfie of the two of you that he posted from your last date. From the looks of things, you two should be more than "just dating." Your friends keep asking you when it is going to happen. It should be any day now, right?

But how do you know for sure that you're officially a "couple"? If there are pictures, posts, and comments woven throughout each of your respective social media profiles, does that qualify you as "romantically involved"? If you've met his friends and family and he's met yours, is that enough? Like it or not, the honest answer is "no"—these signs, while significant, do not mean that you are in an exclusive relationship. The only way to know for sure that you've gone from dating someone to being in an exclusive relationship with him is to discuss your status with one another. It must be agreed upon in unequivocal terms by both you and the guy you're dating; anything less will lead to forced assumptions and confusion. If he keeps pushing the matter aside or responds in vague terms, take a step back and evaluate: What is he trying to say? How do his actions make you feel? Is this a red flag? Don't let his evasiveness become a tactic to lead you on. After a certain point, uncertainty about your status can make you think the relationship is something it's not, which, if he never intended to date you long-term in the first place, can leave you disappointed and heartbroken.

Make sure you've been dating for at least a month before you broach this topic. Keep in mind all of the previous conversations that you've had in the past. Have they all been lighthearted and surface-level, despite how many dates you've gone on? Or has he been flashing signs that he wants to take your connection to the next level? Being aware of these details can give you an idea of when it's time to begin this conversation. After a series of dates, if you're starting to develop feelings for this guy and you can tell that those feelings are, in fact, mutual, it's best to be direct and up-front. There is no need to sugarcoat or be coy about what you want to know. Be prepared for his decision not to come right away; he may need time to process whether or not a relationship is right for him. You may also need to take time to think things through. Is this what you really want? Be confident that you're ready to take this next step. It could change everything!

DATING PITFALLS TO AVOID ON THE ROAD TO COUPLEDOM

Transitioning from singleness to coupledom can be life changing. How you spend your time is liable to change. Your priorities will shift to accommodate this new person, and that's a good thing!

Yet despite our best efforts, we're all prone to certain unhealthy behaviors when we're making this transition. The desire to leave the dating world behind and enter into a full-blown relationship—mixed with the fear of messing it up and becoming single again—could cause you to dismiss your thoughts and concerns, leaving you susceptible to unwise choices.

In this section, I've identified five major pitfalls daters often encounter on the road to becoming a couple—and how to avoid them.

Losing Yourself in the Relationship

The Pitfall: In a misguided attempt to curry favor with the guy you are dating, you begin to prioritize his tastes, opinions, and values over your own, causing you to lose sight of what matters most—you! Women sometimes contort themselves to fit the mold they believe a man desires out of fear that he will lose interest if they don't. What they're really doing is choosing to value the man more than themselves. Remember, dating has to start with you.

How to Avoid It: Never forget your values and the boundaries you've set for yourself. Stay completely honest about what you like and dislike. It's okay to have a different opinion or to disagree about something; in fact, these discrepancies keep things interesting!

Be sure to spend some time away from your guy, either with friends or alone, to remind yourself of what you like—and of what makes you uniquely you. Take an evening or two each week to stay home and read a book or pamper yourself with a soothing bubble bath. Setting this boundary will protect your personal space and allow you to hold on to the things you used to enjoy when you were still single.

Ditching Your Friends

The Pitfall: You become infatuated with the man you're dating, and he takes up all of your free time. You like how you feel whenever you're around him and, therefore, carve out more and more time to be with him. As a result, you find yourself sacrificing the time that you *used* to spend hanging out with your friends to spend time with your new man. But you are not your true self without your friends! And now, the solid ground upon which your friendships were built is beginning to crumble.

How to Avoid It: Your friends are valuable, and the right guy will respect that. Keep your time with your friends sacred. Set up a time every week, or every other week, to spend one-on-one time with them. Plan a girl's night in (or out)—whatever it takes to ensure that you're having fun and are able to talk to one another about your lives.

When you're with your friends, make sure that you aren't using them just to talk about your burgeoning relationship. Check in on their successes and struggles, as well! Use the same amount of effort to cultivate your existing friendships as you do in your romantic relationship.

Moving Too Fast

The Pitfall: Things are going well. So well, in fact, that you feel as though it's safe to take the next step. But as you rush into this new phase of the relationship—whether it be sexual intimacy or making things official—you may sail by some important and potentially problematic characteristics of the man you're seeing. By moving too fast, you skip out on opportunities to learn more about one another—such as how you each handle stressful situations—and determine how compatible you truly are.

How to Avoid It: Moving too fast is another pitfall that is often driven by fear—fear that you will lose your chance to enjoy a healthy relationship, get married, and have a lifelong companion. Hear me when I say: If this relationship is right for you, time will not work against you. Remember what the Bible teaches us: "For everything there is a season, a time for every activity under heaven" (Ecclesiastes 3:1). Experiencing successes and failures together will strengthen the bond you share and teach you both how to really be there for one another. The more patient you are with your relationship, and the more grace with which you allow your love to grow, the more confident you'll be in your decision to take things to the next level—whatever that level may be.

Getting Too Physical

The Pitfall: You find yourself physically attracted to a man. But as a mature woman, you have set personal boundaries, and where you draw the line with regards to sexual intimacy may be one of them. You might believe that kissing and cuddling are acceptable displays of affection in the early stages of a relationship, but that having sex is not. However, because you are *really* into this man, the lines you'd previously drawn may have started to shift. Before you know it, you are crossing a boundary you never meant to cross at a rate you never anticipated.

How to Avoid It: It's important to understand that your physical desires can certainly get the best of you—especially early on in a relationship, when you're liable to get stuck in the throes of infatuation. Just because you're strong in your faith and have resolved to uphold your limits does not mean that you have the self-control to stop things from going too far when you're feeling aroused and want more. Keep your boundaries sacred. Avoid making out in dark places, hanging out in a bedroom, or dancing provocatively when you're out in public. Any of these actions can lead to the assumption that you are okay with physically wanting more. Say that you have set a boundary to only go so far (for example, if you're choosing to abstain from sex)—the fast-paced make-out session, hanging out in a place where sex can most likely occur, or "twerking" against your date could send mixed signals. Each of them could potentially give off the impression that you are okay with the physical passion and pleasures that each of these things can insinuate. By setting a verbal boundary, then adding a sensual layer of physical exceptions, it only confuses your stance and could affect the relationship as a whole. If you enjoy a warm touch or passionate kiss, just be sure you're in a setting that makes it impossible for those things to turn into something more.

Assuming You Know Him Better Than You Do

The Pitfall: After a few good dates, you start to believe you really know the guy you're dating and understand what he wants, needs, and feels about you. Consequently, you conflate this deep understanding with reciprocated intimacy. Or perhaps, out of a sense of pride and desire to avoid conflict, you assume you know him well enough to preemptively make choices that you believe will please him and strengthen your relationship, only to find that those assumptions are wrong and that the choices you've made have damaged your bond rather than solidified it. The Bible tells us plainly, "Pride leads to disgrace, but with humility comes wisdom" (Proverbs 11:2).

How to Avoid It: No matter how much you like someone, you won't be able to know everything about him after only a few dates. For all you know, he's on a path to friendship, whereas you're heading toward a relationship. It's natural for you to want to predict his needs, but it's also important to resist. Whenever you are unclear about the direction your relationship is moving in or what he's feeling or wants from you, it's always best to ask. The conversation may be challenging or awkward, and the answers you receive may not be satisfactory, but it's far more effective than moving forward with the wrong information. Assumptions can lead you down a trail of misunderstanding. But humbling yourself enough to ask questions can lead to much-needed clarity.

Insights and Affirmations

Insights

- Finding someone you want to date can be difficult. Maintaining a healthy relationship with someone can be even more challenging. Remember to remain honest, open, and mindful of your own needs just as much as his.
- Learning how best to communicate with someone you like (and could potentially love) is critical for establishing a foundation on which to build a long-term relationship.
- Even in the very best of dating circumstances, you can find yourself in a pitfall if you lose sight of yourself and your existing relationships.

Affirmations

- From your first date to the altar, speaking out of love will produce an outcome that will leave a lasting impression (see Ephesians 4:29).
- Staying silent about something that concerns or confuses you will never yield the answers you need to make the right choices in the dating world (see Proverbs 17:28).

"At last!" the man exclaimed. "This one is bone from my bone, and flesh from my flesh! She will be called 'woman,' because she was taken from 'man.'" This explains why a man leaves his father and mother and is joined to his wife, and the two are united into one. GENESIS 2:23–24

Chapter 6

LET'S TALK ABOUT SEX

It's vital, yet forbidden. It surrounds us, yet it's often difficult to discuss. It's been essential since the union of Adam and Eve, yet it continues to be a source of confusion for modern couples. I'm talking, of course, about the elephant in the room: I'm talking about sex.

In this chapter, we'll discuss sex—and everything that comes along with it—in the context of modern dating and Christianity.

SEX, FEMININITY, AND CHRISTIANITY

For as long as anyone can remember, sex has been equal parts tantalizing and scandalizing—and all the more tantalizing for being scandalizing. The act of sex and the cultural mores associated with it have been broken, neglected, twisted, misconstrued, and misinterpreted from one generation to the next. As a Christian, I'm sure you're familiar with many of the rules of the game. I'm also sure, though, that in this day and age, those rules have never seemed harder to follow.

In the past, American girls were, by and large, raised to become modest, God-fearing, and husband-pleasing wives. Beacons of grace and class, they would never dare cross the men in their lives. Naturally, sex was taboo. Claiming to enjoy sex, or even implying that you *might* enjoy sex, in terms of how you dressed or behaved, was frowned upon. It simply wasn't the norm.

Until the sexual revolution, that is. The second-wave feminists of the 1960s and '70s enshrined sex as an individual freedom that women had a right to enjoy as much as men, regardless of marital status. Sex could be pleasurable, certainly. But it could also be empowering. In the fight for equal rights, sex was both a means to an end and the end itself—an act of political expression and personal liberation.

In the decades that followed, sex became more casual among younger generations. Madonna and other female iconoclasts, as well as popular movies and TV shows of the era, made sex more mainstream and acceptable to the everyday girl. And as those girls grew up to become women who pursued careers with the same ambition as their male peers, the prototypical nuclear family—complete with the breadwinning husband and domestic housewife—became less common.

These days, sex is everywhere, all the time—not only in the clothes we wear, the songs we listen to, and the movies we watch, but also in the palm of our hands as we scroll through images on the internet or Instagram. Technology aside, the culture at-large has grown more accepting of women—young and old, single and divorced—engaging in "casual sex" with whomever they choose. "Hook ups," facilitated by sex-positive dating apps, are pervasive. Perhaps even more than the act itself, sex, like so many aspects of modern life, has become a way for people to assert and express their identity. If feeling sexy—in terms of whatever "sexy" means to you—makes you feel confident, empowered, and attractive, then it makes sense to incorporate that feeling into your lifestyle choices.

In light of so much progressive change, Christian ways of thinking are often considered "old-fashioned." You may have, for example, been taught that sex before marriage is a big no-no. However, women are increasingly focused on their own education and careers, attending college at higher rates (and accumulating the student debt to match). As a result, the desire to get married and start a family has become less urgent—and often less economically viable. By and large, marriage is no longer a sacred step that must be taken in order to experience pleasing and liberating love. And while many women out there certainly want to get married someday, the exact date is not a determining factor with regards to when they choose to have sex. Ultimately, the traditional pressures to save oneself for marriage have been flipped on their head—nowadays, many women feel pressured to do the exact opposite.

What are the challenges for the Christian woman who wants to wait to have sex until marriage? And, by contrast, what are the challenges for the Christian woman who chooses not to wait, yet still wants to be a good Christian? While Christians are always talking about what not to do and the consequences of disobeying the rules, not a lot of context is provided as to why sex should be saved for marriage in the first place.

In the pages that follow, we'll take a closer look at the intersections of sex and Christianity. It is not my place to say what's right and wrong or how you should choose to reconcile your personal faith and sexuality. It is my hope, however, to provide some valuable insights that will support you in whatever choices you make.

HOW THE BIBLE VIEWS SEX

Simply put, the Bible teaches Christians not to engage in any sexual activity before marriage. To do otherwise is considered an act of "sexual immorality." The Bible states, "But because there is so much sexual immorality, each man should have his own wife, and each woman should have her own husband" (1 Corinthians 7:2). In other words, marriage is what saves us from sexual immorality. "Run from sexual sin! No other sin so clearly affects the body as this one does. For sexual immorality is a sin against your own body" (1 Corinthians 6:18). Sounds pretty harsh. Still, it doesn't stop many Christians from committing "sexual sin."

Putting the Bible aside for a moment, why is sex outside of marriage so dishonorable? For years, Christians have endorsed sexual purity as the key to a fulfilling marriage; if you broke the rules along the way, you wouldn't get the happily-ever-after. But if God created us as sexual beings, why is sex outside of the context of marriage such an awful thing to experience? What does sex really mean to God?

Sex Is Never "Just Sex"

At the beginning of the book of Genesis, God created Eve to be "united into one" with Adam (Genesis 2:23–24). The Bible explains that Eve was created not only to serve as a teammate to Adam but also to become one with him. At first glance, this seems to refer to the act of sexual intercourse. But when you break it down even further, uniting with another person to become "one" carries much more weight than sex.

When you merge two people together to form one person, you cannot just single out sexual organs. You have to consider the mind, the heart, and everything that makes that united person unique. Therefore, sex is never really "just sex." Every time you have sex with someone, you are "uniting into one" with them. In other words, you are combining an emotional and mental level of oneness, along with two bodies literally fitting together. For this reason, sex is much more than a physical act.

Consider what the Bible tells us: "Now Adam had sexual relations with his wife, Eve, and she became pregnant. When she gave birth to Cain, she said, 'With the Lord's help, I have produced a man!'" (Genesis 4:1). However, when you look up the Hebrew meaning of the phrase, "had sexual relations"—Hebrew being the original language in which the Old Testament was written—you'll see that the phrase is translated from the word, *yada*, which means "to know." So, when Adam "had sexual relations" with Eve, it wasn't simply physical: To have sex with her was to *know* her.

Whenever two people engage in sex, their minds, bodies, and hearts connect on a deep and intimate level, whether they realize it or not (which certainly puts "meaningless" one-night stands into perspective). This is all by God's design, and it's why He stated that sex should only be done within marriage; an emotional, mental, and physical connection at this level should only be achieved when you're in love with the one person with whom you decide to be intimate.

Sex Goes Beyond Procreation

God instructed Adam and Eve to have sex: "Be fruitful and multiply. Fill the earth and govern it. Reign over the fish in the sea, the birds in the sky, and all the animals that scurry along the ground" (Genesis 1:28). So naturally, when most people think of sex, they do so in terms of procreation.

Of course, procreation isn't always an option. Some married couples may decide they don't want kids; others may not be physically capable of procreating in the first place. No matter who you are, age will kick in eventually, and menopause will run its course. This doesn't mean that these couples shouldn't practice and enjoy sex. Sex goes beyond procreation. So, why do people choose to have sex in the first place?

According to Scripture, "The husband should fulfill his wife's sexual needs, and the wife should fulfill her husband's needs. The wife gives authority over her body to her husband, and the husband gives authority over his body to his wife" (1 Corinthians 7:3–4). Clearly, men and women both have sexual needs that require fulfillment—needs that go beyond the duty to procreate.

What do some of those needs look like? They could be any number of things: pleasure, closeness, an all-encompassing expression of love with someone you know better than anyone else. While holding someone's hand may give you a sense of these feelings, for others, there are needs that only sex can fulfill. The longer you wait to fulfill them, the more tempted you may become to find a quicker solution. Having sex can distort your perception of a man. But *not* having sex can, too—particularly if your body is willing to expedite a process that your heart and mind are not.

God created us to experience the desire to seek out a certain closeness and intimacy in another that can only be achieved through sex. For this reason, sex is special, and it should be valued as such.

Sex and Marriage

God designed sex to be enjoyed *and* to serve a purpose. Because sex is meant to satisfy a plethora of needs—not merely physical ones—it's safe to say that sex is deeper, more meaningful, and more powerful than the average American may think.

Even so, God intended for sex to be practiced within the walls of marriage. Though the reasons why a woman might choose not to get married or put off getting married are abundant (see "Sex, Femininity, and Christianity" on page 112), those reasons have no bearing on the validity of God's original plan.

Remember, God also planned for us to live without sin and enjoy the bounties of the Garden of Eden forever and ever, and we all know how that turned out. The serpent lied and convinced Eve to eat the fruit from the tree of the knowledge of good and evil; she sinned and convinced Adam to commit the same sin, and both were expelled from the Garden of Eden (Genesis 2:15–3:24). The plan was not to sin, yet sin we do—and God still forgives us, loves us, and draws us back to Him.

Clearly, there are competing viewpoints on sex before marriage in Christianity. Let's explore both of them here.

SAVING YOURSELF FOR MARRIAGE

If you have decided to save yourself for marriage, you are aligning your beliefs with the Scriptures that tell us, "God's will is for you to be holy, so stay away from all sexual sin" (1 Thessalonians 4:3). Even if this is biblically the right thing to do, it is not always easy! For many reasons—the desire to fulfill sexual needs, wanting to express love to someone, and societal realities and pressures, to name only a few—saving yourself for marriage is no longer the popular choice.

But doing something the way God intended has its rewards. Making the decision to wait protects you from getting too close to a man who is not, or may not become, your husband. In this way, you're reserving your heart, body, and mind for someone you are meant to spend your life with, for better or worse, 'til death do you part. On a more practical level, saving yourself also prevents you from having children outside the bonds of marriage and keeps you safe from the spread of sexually transmitted infections and diseases.

Choosing to save yourself for marriage is what God wants for you. He doesn't want this for you because He wants to rule over you and take away your sexual freedom as a woman. Rather, He wants you to experience sex as He designed it: a safe, pleasurable, deep, fulfilling, and intimate experience with a man who longs to be with you, love you, and *know* you more completely than anyone else on Earth.

If you are choosing to save yourself for marriage, I would implore you to be careful not to let go of your purity of mind and heart, either. Just because you choose not to engage in sex doesn't mean that your thoughts or actions *outside* of sex remain pure. God wants you to remain pure, period. The best way to ensure this purity in your love life is to love the way God teaches us to love (see chapter 1) and to honor your values and intentions (see chapters 2 and 3).

"AM I STILL A GOOD CHRISTIAN IF I HAVE SEX BEFORE MARRIAGE?"

I'm going to be real with you. My marriage is absolutely great. My wedding night was fabulous. And . . . I had sex before marriage. Before I met my husband, knowing that I had a sex life before marriage really bothered me. I believed that, because I had not saved myself, I would somehow suffer the consequences once I got married.

But we should not allow thoughts like these to overpower God's truth. Scripture says, "This means that anyone who belongs to Christ has become a new person. The old life is gone; a new life has begun!" (2 Corinthians 5:17).

Jesus died on the cross for us so that *if we choose* to live a Christian life, then whatever happened in our past will be erased for good. If you've engaged in premarital sex but decide later on to save yourself for marriage, God will honor that! Even if it's the week before your wedding, God will honor it. The condition of your heart is what God is focused on, not your sexual history. He's not looking back. You shouldn't, either.

Of course, as I mentioned previously, sex is never "just sex," and if you decide to have sex before marriage, there may be some consequences, particularly if you do not practice safe sex.

Having an honest discussion with your potential husband will bring to light truths that could help you avoid damaging your marriage in the future. It's a hard conversation to have, but it will help establish a strong foundation for both you and your future husband to stand on—with Christ at the center. Ultimately, your marriage will be blessed if you decide to include Christ in it. And that is what makes you a good Christian.

Practical Wisdom: Avoiding Temptation

If you're dating someone who is showing you love at a level (or rate) of intensity that you've never experienced before, it's only natural that your heart, mind, and body will want to reciprocate that love or even take it further. Everyone runs into temptation, and sexual temptations are no different.

If you're not careful, though, temptation can lead you down a path you hadn't planned on taking. Flirting can go too far. Kissing can go too far. A warm hug could lead to a soft caress, and, before you know it, hands are all over the place. Even if you decide to date online, what you see, hear, say, and do on the internet can cause you to overstep your sexual boundaries.

The Bible instructs us to, "Run from anything that stimulates youthful lusts. Instead, pursue righteous living, faithfulness, love, and peace. Enjoy the companionship of those who call on the Lord with pure hearts" (2 Timothy 2:22).

How can you accomplish this in the modern, sex-saturated world of dating and love? As I outlined in chapter 3, setting boundaries is crucial for keeping your actions—and the actions of the person you're dating—in check. Now, let's get specific about a few steps you can take to avoid giving into sexual temptation, regardless of where your personal boundaries may lay.

Set a physical limit. This is not an objective limit, but one you set according to what you personally can handle when it comes to kissing, touching, and other physical acts of affection. Are you ready to kiss someone on the lips in the first place, or should you refrain from kissing entirely? If you kiss a man on the lips, would you also want him to kiss your neck? Does a warm hug last a little longer than usual? Does enjoying a kiss with tongue make you want to delve into a full-on make-out session? Can a harmless back massage turn into a full-body invasion? Know what your own limits are. If you start to feel nervous, uneasy, or uncomfortable, then stand up, leave the room, take a time-out from physically engaging with one another, or change the activity so that you can reset the mood. Do whatever you feel would best bring you back to a place of peace and comfort.

Consciously establishing these limits will help you stay true to them. Of course, it's okay to adjust your limits over time as you both grow closer to one another, as long as you both feel comfortable moving in that direction. If you believe that your values and boundaries are intact, you and your boyfriend can determine how to recalibrate your physical limits together.

Use a code word. If you are out with your date and he does something that turns you on, you can designate a word that either of you can use to let the other know that they should stop doing whatever it is they're doing. Perhaps he casually licks his lips, holds you by your waist, or whispers something sexually suggestive in your ear. Using your established code word will let him know where you stand while keeping things on the down low if, for example, you're out with your friends.

Now, if you agree to enforce this step to keep you both from crossing your sexual boundaries, but your boyfriend is flirtatiously continuing to do the particular things that turn you on, you have a choice to make. You can explain that his actions are disrespectful of you and your boundaries, or you can choose to do nothing and allow him to woo you toward shifting your limit when you feel the time is right.

Do not meet alone at each other's homes. Hanging out at home can be comfortable and cost-effective, but it can also lead to the two of you getting a little *too* comfortable. Ever heard of the phrase, "Netflix and chill"? There's a reason why relaxing in one's personal space can make you fall prey to temptation. You're in the comfort of your (or his) own home. No one is watching. Anything is possible. Be very careful in this setting and avoid it entirely if you're not sure you can resist crossing the boundaries you've set for yourself.

HOW MEN VIEW SEX

When discussing communication in chapter 5, I mentioned that men are wired differently than women. This is especially true when it comes to sex. Typically, women are more driven to have sex for its emotional rewards, while men tend to be more drawn to sex for what they can get out of it physically. This does not mean that all men are barbaric creatures (or that *no* women are); in general, though, it is simply how God made us.

It's also how our culture has *shaped* us. In the media, women are hypersexualized from a young age, advertised as covetable objects of male desire. On the other hand, outdated notions of masculinity socialize men to believe women are created for their pleasure, with needs subservient to their own—a belief that is perpetuated by pornography and that lies at the root of many of the abusive behaviors brought to light by the long-overdue #MeToo movement.

A man's self-worth is often tethered to his strength and power—consider the predominantly male preoccupations with weight lifting and contact sports—which is itself bound up in making sexual "conquests." Whereas women are traditionally taught to withhold their sexuality, men are pressured to seek out sex at an earlier age and as often as possible.

Certainly, times are changing, and it's not fair to say that all men—or even *most* men—subscribe to these kinds of beliefs and behavior. But is this old-fashioned yet persistent way of thinking how God teaches men to love? Absolutely not.

Like women, men are taught to love in the same manner God has shown us: to love sacrificially, to serve the needs of others, and to love with an intimacy that goes beyond the physical pleasures of sex. However, everyone experiences sexual temptation. What a man chooses to do with it has consequences—good and bad—for both himself and the person he chooses to date.

In the following section, I've highlighted three examples of men from the Bible worth considering when it comes to men, dating, and sex.

Joseph (Genesis 39–41)

Joseph was sold into slavery by his 11 older brothers. During his time as a slave in Egypt, he caught the eye of his master's wife. She would throw herself at him and insist that he lie with her. Joseph refused and fled the scene. He did not give in to the temptations of sex. Later, God chose Joseph to become Pharaoh's right-hand man, and he rose in power, blessings, and God's favor.

Sometimes, a man will decide to remain pure and righteous. Although you may feel you need to give in to your sexual temptations, the man you are with may honor his commitment to you and to God. That is a man worth keeping!

David (2 Samuel 11–12:25)

David is known for being a man "after God's own heart" (1 Samuel 13:14). He sought the Lord through the good and the bad, yet there was one thing he did that led him down the wrong path: He committed adultery with a married woman.

Adultery is considered to be as sinful as having sex before marriage (see Mark 7:20–23). And the King of Israel, handpicked by God Himself, chose to commit this act. Did that make David a good follower of God? Not necessarily. But what David did afterward gave him a second chance to make things right: He turned to God.

Sometimes, men will set boundaries, declare intentions, and honor values, but they will still give in to sexual temptation. What they choose to do afterward is what matters most. If you and the man you're dating have crossed the sexual boundaries you had decided to set earlier in your relationship, talk to him. What you both decide to do afterward will affect your relationship moving forward. Will you choose to reset your boundaries? Will you both turn to God to receive His love? Or will you choose to allow shame, guilt, or fear into your relationship?

Remember, God loves you both and wants to see you succeed! Going to Him together when sexual tension, temptation, or struggles arise will help you create a relationship grounded in God's grace and love.

Amnon (2 Samuel 13:1–22)

Amnon, the son of King David, was in love with his half sister, Tamar. He became so infatuated with her that he pretended to be sick so she would take care of him. But when they were alone together, he forced himself on her. Afterward, the Bible says, "He hated her even more than he had loved her" (2 Samuel 13:15). Tamar's future was ruined because she was raped, and their family was torn apart because of Amnon's actions.

Here's the truth: There are some guys out there who have no desire for you whatsoever other than to have sex with you. They will say whatever it is they need to say just to get you into bed. Men can use their power and position to place you in harmful or destructive circumstances. Their behavior can lead to sexual harassment, assault, or rape.

For these reasons, it is very important that you protect yourself at all times. Set your boundaries, especially when you are meeting with someone for the first time. Trust your gut and be mindful of where the conversation goes and how your date reacts in different situations, particularly when they're laced with sexual temptation.

For additional resources on sexual assault, please refer to the Resources section (page 151).

Insights and Affirmations

Insights

- Likely, the Bible has been telling you what to think about sex for a long time. But what you choose to do is between you and God.
- Sex is much deeper, more intimate, and more personal than the media often portrays it to be. For this reason, God originally designed it to be experienced when one reaches the highest relationship possible: marriage.
- Men may desire sex for different reasons than women, but the temptations to pursue it, and the opportunities to flee from those temptations, are the same.

Affirmations

- Marriage is part of God's plan: a covenant partnership where one knows the other completely, lovingly, and wholeheartedly. Marriage is a relationship in which shame is not welcome (Genesis 2:25).
- As a Christian, your body is God's temple, and He dwells within your heart, ready to love and receive you just as you are (1 Corinthians 6:19–20).

He heals the brokenhearted and bandages their wounds. He counts the stars and calls them all by name. How great is our Lord! His power is absolute! His understanding is beyond comprehension! PSALM 147:3–5

Chapter 7

BREAKING UP AND BOUNCING BACK

As much as you might not want to think about it, breaking up is a frequent byproduct of getting together. Sometimes, breakups are healthy and neat; other times, they're hostile and messy. One thing is for certain: Nobody wants to experience a breakup! But when you finally overcome the heartache and find your groove again, you can re-emerge into the dating scene stronger (and more knowledgeable) than you were before.

In this chapter, I'll break down the breakup process: how to handle a breakup, how to lean on God in the aftermath, and how to get back out there.

BREAKING UP IS HARD TO DO

Nobody wants to admit they were a part of something that failed. Breakups are so hard precisely because they can make you feel like you've failed at love—when in reality, all that has failed is the relationship. At the end of the day, everyone wants to find love and a successful relationship. When you break up, it's natural to feel like love is, indeed, the stuff of fairy tales and rom-coms—that it simply isn't meant for you.

It's critical to remember that going through a breakup doesn't mean that something is wrong with you or that you aren't capable of experiencing love. In some cases, a breakup is downright necessary to protect your heart and preserve your well-being. You might find yourself in an unhealthy relationship where you are totally dependent on your significant other to feel happy, healthy, and whole (this may be a sign of a behavioral condition known as *codependency*). Perhaps your partner is overprotective, controlling, or, worse, physically or emotionally abusive.

All of the above are pressing reasons to get out of a relationship. If you're afraid of how your partner might respond, try to end things in a public place so that you are not endangered or made to feel threatened. If conditions feel particularly dangerous, consider bringing a friend or two for support. Ultimately, breaking up over the phone might be the best option in such cases. If you're living with someone with whom you have an unhealthy relationship, have an escape plan—make sure your bags are packed and you have somewhere to stay before you break things off so you can leave and never look back. If his pattern of abuse has left you afraid for your physical well-being or life, I encourage you to consider seeking a restraining order or reporting the abuse to your local police department. Your own safety should *never* be jeopardized by a breakup.

With most relationships, however, the breakup is mutual—or, at the very least, uncontentious. Perhaps you've both just had a change of heart; perhaps you love each other, but you're not *in* love with each other (there's a difference!). While there are no hard feelings, you've simply acknowledged that the relationship isn't going anywhere and that you are better off going your separate ways. If this is the case, it is best for you to address the issue and break up sooner rather than later, lest you waste more of each other's time.

This is easier said than done. It's likely that you care deeply for this person and will want to put off hurting them for as long as possible. And if you've been together for a long time—and share things more tangible than memories—it can be a daunting task to extricate yourself; it can feel like starting over, in more ways than one. But the longer you keep the relationship going once you know it's over, the more you run the risk of really hurting each other when you finally break things off. You may stop caring for him altogether or even find someone else you're interested in getting to know. What could have been a sad, yet respectful parting could, instead, become a full-blown breakup explosion.

The most challenging breakup, of course, is a divorce. In the past, there was a stigma surrounding divorce. Nowadays, they're quite common—according to the American Psychological Association, about

40 to 50 percent of marriages in the United States end in divorce. Still, judgment lingers whenever a couple gets a divorce. In particular, Christians view divorce as something that is not godly, yet there are as many divorces among Christians as there are among non-Christians.

Regardless of whether you've gone through a breakup or a divorce, these situations are not the be-all and end-all for finding love. God will always love you, and He longs to heal you from those heartbreaking moments. No matter what happened during your breakup, God still wants you to trust Him as you move forward (see Psalm 34:17–18).

You may not want to hear this, but securing a partner who satisfies your needs, wants, values, and desires may require you to experience a few breakups along the way. But think of it this way: If you're serious about finding the right guy to love you, breakups aren't really failures—they're merely stepping-stones on the path to a successful, lifelong relationship.

A BROKEN HEART ONLY COMES BACK STRONGER

As much as breakups are an (almost) unavoidable obstacle in the dating world, make no mistake, they can leave you feeling extremely distraught! Whether you're the one initiating the breakup or someone has broken up with you, the experience can leave you wallowing in a pool of intensely unpleasant emotions.

Like most women, I've experienced my fair share of heartache. There was the time when the guy I was dating didn't trust me at all. All the time we spent together was wasted on me trying to prove to him that I was worth his trust. The breakup was frustrating. I reached a point where I wanted out, yet he fought hard to keep us together.

Then, there was the time when I was with someone who started to develop unhealthy habits behind my back. His lack of self-care caused me to work overtime just to keep us together. In the end, his toxicity won, and he broke up with me. Can you believe it? The breakup left me feeling humiliated for months, considering how hard I'd worked to keep the relationship together.

Or, how about the time I was so into a guy that I truly thought he would become my husband? He broke up with me over the phone after two years of dating for being "too clingy." After him came the rebound who never took our "relationship" seriously, followed by the cheater who said all the things I wanted to hear just to draw me closer, only to completely ignore me until the next time he wanted more attention.

Breakup after breakup after breakup. After one too many of those, you start to feel . . . well, broken. It's frustrating to feel like no matter what you do or how much you open up, you're never going to experience a successful relationship. As a result, your self-esteem suffers; if you're not careful, depression can slink in under the cover of darkness. Before you know it, you're allowing your pain from the past and desperation for a brighter future to rule your love life. Resentment festers—not just for your ex but for men in general. Fear robs you of peace as you wonder if you'll ever find love again. All hope is lost. Your faith is faint. And so, you stop trying to look for the right relationship because you've come to realize that the right relationship does not exist.

At least, that's what I used to believe. And that was how I used to feel. It wasn't until I began to believe in God's truth that I snapped out of my breakup blues. "God causes everything to work together for the good of those who love God and are called according to his purpose for them" (Romans 8:28). This truth was a silver lining: *Perhaps all those breakups were in service of something more.* Maybe, just maybe, buried beneath all that pain, there was an underlying lesson I needed to learn about myself and the relationship I truly wanted.

The breakup I had with the guy who had trust issues taught me that I shouldn't have to prove myself for a guy to fully love and accept me. That brand of insecurity is like cancer to any relationship.

The breakup I had with the toxic, unhealthy guy taught me that I cannot save anyone who doesn't want to save himself and that I deserve to be in a relationship with someone who is healthy and honest.

I learned that being too clingy is never good for anybody and that if I'm looking solely to a man for my peace and happiness, then the person I really need to work on is myself. I learned that rebounds are never serious, cheaters don't deserve a moment of my time, and I am worthy of love and a genuine relationship.

Wherever you are in your breakup story, whether it just happened two weeks ago or you are still feeling the effects of what happened six years ago, please know that those negative emotions are valid and shouldn't be ignored. That surge of sadness, that rush of anger, that fear, regret, or even resentment—they're all strong side effects of a breakup. You shouldn't suppress these emotions, but you also shouldn't carry them into your next relationship.

Ultimately, those emotions are jagged pieces of your grieving process for your ex and for your relationship. Yes, that's right: When you break up, you enter a period of grief. And just as you must learn to cope with the loss of a loved one, you now must learn how to cope with the loss of this relationship. Remember what the Bible tells us: "The Lord hears his people when they call to him for help. He rescues them from all their troubles. The Lord is close to the brokenhearted; he rescues those whose spirits are crushed" (Psalm 34:17–18).

Though you may seem broken, you are not lost. God is there to restore you and your broken heart. Those feelings won't last forever, so long as you choose to let them go.

The Power of Letting Go

Letting go of someone you once had (and maybe still have) very strong feelings for can be devastating. It requires you to turn away from something you once so fervently believed in: the relationship, and the man you may have thought you'd spend forever with.

It takes a lot of guts to leave something like that behind. I applaud you! While it may not have seemed like the right (or easy) action to take in the moment, take a step back and look at the bigger picture. Letting go of a man who may not have had your best interest at heart is actually a powerful act of self-love. It is

Practical Wisdom: How to Cope with a Breakup

You don't have to enter a downward spiral filled with stereotypical pints of heartache-related ice cream to get through a breakup (although *some* ice cream never hurts).

Here are some healthier ways to cope:

Talk to someone. This could be friends, a family member, God (through prayer), or a professional counselor. Sharing your pain, your fears, and the effects of the breakup will help you process everything you're feeling without internalizing it.

Focus on yourself. Give yourself a new wardrobe, a new makeup look, or even a different hairstyle! Spend some time getting yourself to a healthy place: Eat healthy foods, get enough sleep, and engage in more physical activity.

Journal. Journaling is a great way to get all of your thoughts out in a safe and nonjudgmental way. Use journaling to vent, process, and share the honest truth about how you feel.

Embrace how you're really feeling. It's okay to not feel okay. You are allowed to cry and feel sad, even if the breakup was a good thing. You cannot control how you feel, so embrace it instead. Give yourself permission to feel your feelings. If you don't, you'll run the risk of suppressing them, turning them into baggage that you'll carry with you into your next relationship.

tantamount to an affirmation—that you are prioritizing your heart, your wants, and your needs ahead of anyone else's.

Of course, after a breakup, you will be periodically tempted to return to what once made you happy. You may entertain the thought of striking up conversations with your ex, just for the attention; upon seeing a movie or hearing a song that reminds you of him, you may feel the urge to reach out and reminisce. In moments like these, remember why you broke up in the first place, and remain steadfast in your decision. Be careful not to place your ex on a pedestal. While you may find yourself looking back fondly on the good times, the truth is there were plenty of bad times, too. Do not cast those aside.

To make it easier on yourself, it might be best to unfollow your ex on social media, at least temporarily, or restrict his privileges so that his current activity doesn't surprise you the next time you open up Facebook or Instagram. Depending on the severity of the breakup, you may want to block his phone number to avoid receiving any text messages. If you run in the same social circles, perhaps try to visit your routine places at different times so you don't accidentally run into each other. And while this step could be the most difficult, it may be best to return or rid yourself of his belongings. Though he is gone, his scent on his sweatshirt may still linger, and holding on to it doesn't help you move on any faster.

In the end, it's hard to neglect the fact that you once believed this guy would give you the happiness and fulfillment you longed for. But during this period of uncertainty, it's critical to remember God's truth: "Those who know your name trust in you, for you, O Lord, do not abandon those who search for you" (Psalm 9:10). The man you loved may have let you down, but God's love never will.

Naturally, then, one of the most effective ways of letting go of your ex is by redirecting your faith and focus back to God. Believe that God has something better planned for you not just because God is good but because you are good, too! Remind yourself to let God in while everything else is fading out, because God's love is better and more fulfilling than any other love out there. Remind yourself that self-love means making the tough calls when they're necessary, because your values deserve to be appreciated. Lastly, remind yourself that there is no perfect man! But there is a man out there who is better than the man you are trying to distance yourself from.

So, do yourself a favor: *Believe in yourself enough to give love another chance.* Not just any love, but the love that God has intended for you to enjoy to the fullest.

Moving On

During your relationship, you realized something was off. Your values were not being honored. Or your boundaries were crossed. Or your boyfriend no longer exemplified the kind of traits you look for in a man. In any event, you felt as if your future happiness was being taken from you, and you had to do what you had to do. The decision was made. The breakup happened. Your once boyfriend is now your ex. Hopefully, you've started to learn to let go, but letting go is only half of the equation. How on earth do you move on? How can you transition from a life you once shared with someone special to life as a single woman again?

Following a breakup, your emotions are typically in overdrive, and it's tough to try to carry on when you're feeling down and out. For this reason, you may linger in the "breakup zone" longer than you intend to. It sounds so simple, but the first step to moving on is to actually make the decision to move on! You have to want it. You have to be willing to let go of "what once was" and decide that you are ready to move toward "what could be."

To get yourself in this mindset, you must begin to steer clear of the negative thoughts and feelings you may harbor toward your ex. I know it sounds crazy, but hurt people will continue to hurt people. If you want to move on, you eventually need to heal. As I mentioned before, it's healthy to embrace your feelings. However, you must not luxuriate in them. The Bible teaches us to "get rid of all bitterness, rage, anger, harsh words, and slander, as well as all types of evil behavior. Instead, be kind to each other, tenderhearted, forgiving one another, just as God through Christ has forgiven you" (Ephesians 4:31–32).

You may have to pray that God will help you forgive your ex and show you how to let go of the pain you amassed during the breakup. You may even feel a bit of anger toward God Himself for allowing you to go through what you went through. But once you are able to come to terms with the past, practice forgiveness and kindness, and trust that God is *for* you and not against you (Romans 8:31), you'll be able to focus on taking healthy steps forward.

And take it from me: Moving on from a past relationship does not mean you are starting over in the dating world. Quite the contrary! Now, you have another valuable experience under your belt. You know with greater clarity what you want and what you need, what works and what doesn't. Think back to the relationship that just ended. What was good about it? What was bad? Which of your ex's behaviors drew you closer to him? Which of his behaviors pushed you away? Conversely, which of your own behaviors drew him closer and pushed him away? Perhaps these are the kinds of behaviors you'll want to keep in mind when someone new comes along. Keep track of the good stuff, book-mark the bad, and carry this information with you into the next phase of your love life.

What's the Word?

Don't be afraid, for I am with you. Don't be discouraged, for I am your God. I will strengthen you and help you. I will hold you up with my victorious right hand.
ISAIAH 41:10

Experiencing a heartbreak can make you feel weak, inside and out. Mentally, you are drained and stuck in feelings of hopelessness, hurt, and maybe even humiliation. Emotionally, you are confused because your feelings of love and closeness have likely been replaced with resentment and heartache. Breakups can even take a physical toll; anger, stress, and depression can all leave their mark as you do whatever it takes to keep it together.

In times like these, look toward God and His truth. For it is in this exact moment of weakness that God will strengthen you and help you. While it may look different to everyone, make no mistake, you will feel God's power over you and be able to make it through the day. Every day after that, with God as your guide, it will get easier. He will give you the courage, peace, and rest to get through this season.

You may believe you'll never stop crying over your pain or feel joy and happiness ever again, but God will provide strength! He will find ways to make you smile and feel loved. He will bring family, friends, and others into your life to remind you that you are okay and that this, too, shall pass. One night, you may not be able to sleep because you're too busy thinking about your ex; the next, you may feel such peace that you end up sleeping like a baby! It's in moments like those that God is fortifying you to endure this period in your life and preparing you to move into a new one.

So, look to Him. Do not be afraid in this time. Have faith in God and His encouraging words!

OPENING YOURSELF
UP TO LOVE AGAIN

You've been healing, growing, looking to God, and loving yourself. It's been an amazing journey, and the transformation has been beautiful. After what may have felt like forever, you no longer feel the aftershocks of your breakup. Things are starting to look up. Good for you!

As you embrace this moment, be careful not to let fear get in the way of your progress. It's time to entertain the idea of opening yourself up to love again.

I know, I know. You just did that, and you got burned. But let's go back to the beginning: It's hard to find the right person if you're not open to the world! In order to grow in this area of your life—in order to experience a loving companionship with a man who honors you and fits your ideal traits and values—you have to be willing to step out of your comfort zone again. It may be hard, but you have to be willing to put yourself out there.

Of course, there is no objective timeline for how long it takes to mend a broken heart. Likewise, there is no exact timeframe for how long you may choose to refrain from dating to work on yourself (despite what some pushy friends and relatives may tell you). You have to do what's best for you, and only you know what that entails.

You'll know that you're absolutely ready to open yourself up again when you feel at peace about it. Do not respond to external pressures; rather, look inside yourself to determine whether dating is something you actively want to pursue. There will come a time when you are feeling your best and the desire to share that joyous space with someone else will lodge itself in your heart. Not out of a desperate longing, but out of a sense of readiness. In that moment, you'll know you're ready, and you'll be in the right headspace to search for love with a clear heart and calm mind, free from fear and bitterness.

Baby Steps

The Bible encourages you to "fix your thoughts on what is true, and honorable, and right, and pure, and lovely, and admirable. Think about things that are excellent and worthy of praise" (Philippians 4:8). So, when you feel at peace and want to search for love again, do it with an intention that will align your actions with your desired outcomes. You want a relationship that will last. One that values who you are and what you believe in. A relationship with a man who isn't marred by deal breakers, but one who is willing to pursue you and all that you embody.

As you adjust your thoughts to match your attitude, remember the basics we've discussed: Frequent the places you love. Have fun with friends and explore the hobbies, activities, and events that bring you joy! Make a list of all of people, places, and activities that make you happy and start spending your free time indulging in them. Start a walking routine in your favorite park.

Buy a new journal and write one page each morning. Learn a new recipe every week. Call your parents (or grandparents) once a week to reconnect. These are just a few ideas to get your wheels turning.

Though it's comfortable to start off alone in the comfort of your own home, find ways to indulge your passions publicly, perhaps through a class, event, or group setting with friends. Join a monthly book club. Look into the fitness classes your closest gym or rec center offers and commit to going for the next month. Instead of heading home, enjoy your coffee at your local café as you read a book, journal, or simply people watch. Even if you're not quite in the mood, make a point of saying "yes" to outgoing experiences with your friends that sound like fun, such as bowling, karaoke night, or a painting party!

Additionally, use this opportunity to dive into something completely new. Stretch yourself beyond that comfort zone! Be daring. Be bold. Try new things. Redouble your efforts toward achieving a goal you may have left by the wayside during your last relationship. As you take measures to explore new places and sides of yourself, new people will enter your life, as well.

And if you believe you are ready to meet someone new, only to discover that you aren't comfortable yet, don't worry! It's okay to take baby steps. Keep in contact through text. Go on a few daytime dates or enjoy some group outings with friends, where you invite the guy to tag along. Test the waters by getting to know him as you take in how you're feeling with the thought of getting serious. If you're anxious or uncomfortable with the prospect of moving into a relationship, let him know that while a relationship is something you eventually want, it simply isn't a good time. You're allowed to remain friends with someone you like while you continue to heal and grow.

In the meantime, stay focused on you. Keep looking to God as your guide, your peace, your courage, and your strength. Slowly, but surely, you will come around, and when that happens, the timing will be just right.

Wrong Turns

Any time we have to heal, whether it be from a scrape or heartache, we find ourselves exposed to further hurt. We are not completely ourselves yet; we are still raw. And though this vulnerability is key to dating success, it can, in the aftermath of a breakup, leave you increasingly susceptible to making rash decisions—out of fear, impatience, or pain.

These wrong turns can come in many forms. Rarely will they announce themselves as "wrong"—likely, they will feel right at the time. Perhaps you'll choose to partake in behavior you normally wouldn't, such as drinking or excessive flirtation. Perhaps you'll find yourself attracted to the first handsome guy you meet without pausing to consider the important details of his character. If you still haven't fully let go of your ex, perhaps you'll find yourself with a new guy who is just like the old guy. It's easy to end up going in the opposite direction when you try to push a relationship forward faster than you would under typical circumstances. Be patient. Recognize the swirl of emotions that may be influencing your judgments. And act accordingly.

Ultimately, wrong turns happen when you refuse to let yourself heal—when you take matters into your own hands without looking to God as a guide of love. They happen when you decide that you do not want to move on from your past or learn from its difficulties. But wrong turns lead you away from your destination. They'll have you lost in no time. You have the map and a great guide in God. Let Him lead you down a road replete with love, respect, and understanding.

Insights and Affirmations

Insights

- You are never alone after going through a breakup. Not only do you have friends and family in your corner—God will never leave you.
- The greatest thing that can happen from a breakup is that it brings you one step closer to finding the person who's best for you.
- The turning point from grieving to overcoming a breakup is the personal choice you make to heal, grow, and, finally, move on.

Affirmations

- Be thankful for your good and bad relationship experiences; they will make you more faithful toward God's plans for you and your love life (see 1 Thessalonians 5:18).
- Even though breakups are hard to process and hurtful, God uses them to make you stronger and wiser (see James 1:2–4).

RESOURCES

BOOKS

Lady in Waiting: Becoming God's Best While Waiting for Mr. Right by Jackie Kendall and Debby Jones

Relationship Goals: How to Win at Dating, Marriage, and Sex by Michael Todd

101 Questions to Ask Before You Get Engaged by H. Norman Wright

Love, Sex, and Lasting Relationships: God's Prescription for Enhancing Your Love Life by Chip Ingram

How to Get a Date Worth Keeping by Henry Cloud

The 5 Love Languages: The Secret to Love that Lasts by Gary Chapman

The Wait: A Powerful Practice for Finding the Love of Your Life and the Life You Love by DeVon Franklin and Meagan Good

Sex, Purity, and the Longings of a Girl's Heart: Discovering the Beauty and Freedom of God-Defined Sexuality by Kristen Clark and Bethany Beal

Uninvited: Living Loved When You Feel Less Than, Left Out, and Lonely by Lysa TerKeurst

It's Not Supposed to Be This Way: Finding Unexpected Strength When Disappointments Leave You Shattered by Lysa TerKeurst

The Single Woman's Prayer Book: Prayers to Prepare Your Heart & Soul for Love, Romance, and Mr. Right by Selina Almodovar

DOCUMENTARIES

I Survived *I Kissed Dating Goodbye*
youtube.com/watch?v=ybYTkkQJw_M

SEXUAL HEALTH RESOURCES

A Guide to Safer Sex
publichealth.va.gov/docs/womens-health-guide
/safer-sex.pdf

National Sexual Assault Telephone Hotline via RAINN
rainn.org/about-national-sexual-assault-telephone
-hotline

REFERENCES

American Psychological Association. "Marriage & Divorce." Accessed May 12, 2020. apa.org/topics/divorce/.

Anderson, Monica, Emily A. Vogels, and Erica Turner. "The Virtues and Downsides of Online Dating." Pew Research Center. Accessed March 3, 2020. pewresearch.org/internet/2020/02/06/the-virtues-and-downsides-of-online-dating/.

Thottam, Isabel. "10 Online Dating Statistics You Should Know." eharmony. Accessed May 18, 2020. eharmony.com/online-dating-statistics/.

INDEX

rejection, 89–90

trusting your gut, 84–85

wanting a second date, 87

Fitness clubs, working out at, 62

Fitness routine, 23

Friends, 58–59

  connecting with, 23

  coping with a breakup, 138

  dating friends of, 57, 59–60

  pitfall of ditching, 104

Friendship, values, 26

G

Garden of Eden, 5, 10, 118

Genesis 1:28, 116

Genesis 2:15–3:24, 118

Genesis 2:18, 15

Genesis 2:23-24, 110, 115

Genesis 2:25, 128

Genesis 3:15, 5

Genesis 4:1, 116

Genesis 22:1-2, 3

Genesis 39–41 (Joseph),

    sex and, 125

Ghost/ghosting, 34, 67, 89–90

God

  belief in, 43

  comforting heartache, 142–143

  connecting with, 23

  as guide to suitable man, 46

  real love, 2

  trusting, ix–xii

  unconditional love, 4–5

  workmanship in you, 24

God's will, 12–13, 15–16

Gyms, working out at, 62

H

Haircare routine, 23

Hangouts, favorite, for

    meeting, 60–61

"Happily ever after" dreams, ix–x

Happily-ever-afters, ix, 2, 115

Health and wellness, as value, 27

Heartache, 131, 134, 138, 143, 147

Hemsworth, Chris, 40

Hobbies, 23

Honesty

  assessing relationship, 96–97

  conversations, 91–92

  open dialogue about

    your faith, 94–95

  as value, 26

Hook ups, x, 113

I

Immeasurable, love, 6–7

Independence, as value, 26

Infatuation, 49

Insights

  attraction, 51

  breaking up, 149

  communication, 108

  dating, 17

  God's ways, 36

  online dating, 77

  sex, 128

Isaac, 3

Isaiah 41:10, 142

Isaiah 55:8-9, 34, 36

Islam, 47

J

James 1:2-4, 149

James 1:19, 13

James 2:17, 14

James 4:8, 81

Jesus, 5, 40

Job or career, 43

1 John 4:7-8, 17

1 John 4:8, 3

1 John 4:19, 7

John 1:12, 8
Joseph (Genesis 39–41),
    sex and, 125
Joshua 1:9, 52
Journaling
    coping with a breakup, 138
    prayers, 23
    thoughts, 81, 146
    well-being, 22

L

Love, 1, 2–9
    Bible characteristics of, 44
    choice, 8–9
    essential, 7–8
    immeasurable, 6–7
    opening up after
        breakup, 144–148
    sacrifice, 3–4
    trust about, 2–3
    unconditional, 4–5
    yourself first, 20–23
Lust, 49

M

Mark 7:20–23, 126
Marriage
    Christianity and sex, 113–114
    dating and, 82, 97
    God's plan, 15, 17
    saving self (sex) in, ix,
        xi, 30, 45, 49
    sex and, 113, 114–115, 118–120
    unconditional love, 5
Matthew 22:36–40, 7, 11, 17
Meditation, 23
Meeting people. See also
        Online dating
    charitable organization for
        volunteering, 63–64
    church as, 56–57

communal places of
    interest, 60–64
enrolling in a class, 62
favorite hangouts for, 60–61
friends of friends for, 57, 59–60
gym, fitness club or
    yoga studio, 62
joining a club, 61
online, 67–72
participation in cultural
    events, 63
what to do when, 64–65, 67
Men, view of sex, 124–127, 128
Mental well-being, 22, 27
#MeToo movement, 124
Mr. Right, 40, 42

O

Online dating, 67–72
    building and evaluating
        a profile, 72–74
    Bumble, 69
    Christian Mingle, 68
    Coffee Meets Bagel, 69–70
    eharmony, 70
    insights and affirmations, 77
    Our Time, 71
    red flags in, 73–74
    seven commandments of, 74–76
    social media, 71–72
Our Time, 71

P

Past relationships, 84
"Perfect man", 40–41, 51
Personal care, 23
Pew Research Center, 68
Philippians 4:7, 85
Philippians 4:8, 145
Physical attraction. See Attraction
Physical fitness, 44

ACKNOWLEDGMENTS

If I may just start off by giving thanks and glory to God—I remember praying countless prayers about using me and my testimony for His good. He knew about this book way before I did! Even in my darkest hours, when I thought that my work was going unnoticed, He saw it and made this opportunity happen. I thank God for His relentless pursuit for me, my heart, and my purpose to reach His children.

I want to thank my "Hey Girl Hey Gang." You ladies are the ones who have read my words, watched my videos, shared my posts, and kept me going. Your support, emails, comments, and prayers for me and my ministry have been the fuel I needed to push past any inner doubts or insecurities I ever had. You showed me that it was okay to be myself and to create a brand and ministry that reflected that. Thanks for choosing me to encourage you to trust God with your hearts.

To my editor, Sam, for practically holding my hand and walking me through this project step-by-step. Your insightfulness and the fact that you are *not* a Christian woman are what I needed to pull through and address the really tough questions. Together, I believe we created something truly inspiring and great. Thank you.

To Matt Buonaguro and the entire Callisto team, I thank you for taking a chance on me. For helping me take my words and turn them into this amazing book that will be read and shared all across the world! You have opened doors for me that will help me reach new heights and new dreams. It was my honor and a pleasure to work with each of you.

To my amazing New Life Church, friends, and family, thank you for your endless belief in me and my writing. I am forever grateful to have your love surrounding me.

To my babies, William and Solomon, thank you for letting mommy go to work all those days when you wanted me to play cars and dinosaurs instead. I live every day to make you both proud.

Lastly, to my husband, Kyle. You are my biggest cheerleader, my number one fan, and my very best friend. This is for us. Thank God for you. I love you.

ABOUT THE AUTHOR

Selina Almodovar is an author and relationship coach who has helped hundreds of thousands of Christian women across the world rediscover themselves so they can reignite their relationship with God, attract love, and enjoy marriage.

Selina began her ministry in 2012, coaching women on how to reshape their faith and love life. Her first book, *The Single Woman's Prayer Book*, has been sold worldwide and formed a tribe of women who seek to find a fulfilling and satisfying relationship with God at the center. Her second book, *The Engaged Woman's Prayer Book*, took this desire a step further to help women plan a wedding and marriage using God as the foundation for their new season of matrimony.

Along with her prayer books, Selina has created faith-based e-books, online courses, and devotionals for single, dating, and married women. She has been featured on the TCT television show, *Julie and Friends*, as well as several podcasts and international publications.

At home, Selina is a mom to two sons and is happily married to her best friend, Kyle.

Learn more about Selina at SelinaAlmodovar.com.